Vernon God Little

By **DBC Pierre**

Adapted by **Tanya Ronder**

Vernon God Little was first produced at the Young Vic on 8 May 2007
as a co-production with Cuba Pictures

This new production opened at the Young Vic on 27 January 2011

Young Vic

Vernon God Little

By **DBC Pierre**

Adapted by **Tanya Ronder**

Jesus	Luke Brady
Mom	Clare Burt
Lasalle/Dr Goosens/Pelayo	Daniel Cerqueira
Lally	Peter De Jersey
Vernon	Joseph Drake
Pam	Johnnie Fiori
Ella/Taylor	Lily James
Vaine/Leona/Team Leader	Penny Layden
Sheriff Porkorney	Nathan Osgood
Abdini	Duncan Wisbey
Direction	Rufus Norris
Design	Ian MacNeil
Costume	Nicky Gillibrand
Musical Direction and Arrangement	Phil Bateman
Light	Paule Constable with Jane Dutton
Sound	Rich Walsh
Choreography	Lizzi Gee
Show MD	Duncan Wisbey
Casting	Maggie Lunn
Dialect	Michaela Kennen
Assistant Direction	Rikki Henry
Assistant Set Design	Jim Gaffney

Rikki Henry is Jerwood Assistant Director

Stage Manager	Joni Carter
Deputy Stage Manager	Nicole Keighley
Assistant Stage Manager	Sarah Hopkins
Costume Associates	Helen Johnson and Rachel Canning
Assistant Costume Supervisor	Rachael Graham
Wigs and Make-up Supervisor	Anetta Ollerearnshaw
Wardrobe Assistant and Dressers	Morag Hood and Alice Fitzgerald
Wig Dresser	Abbie Bridgman
Makers	Jackie Burston, Will Skeet and Jay Matthews
Dyeing	Nicola Kileen
Glasses	Arckiv
Sound Operator	Sally Evans
Stage Crew	Ben Porter and Mark Richards
Set built by Miraculous Engineering and in Young Vic workshops by	Emma Hayward, Gibson Arpino, Rachaelle Day, Joana Ferrão and Ed Wirtz
Scenic Artist	Charlotte Gainey

 Lead sponsor of the **Young Vic's Funded Ticket Scheme**

With special thanks to Jill Green Casting, Paul Arditti, Duncan Wisbey, Louise Meakes, Karen Wood, Sian Willis, London Fabric Company, Sparks Theatrical Hire, Stage Sound Services, Savilles Stainless and Wanzl for the donation of trolleys

Subsidised rehearsal facilities provided by
JERWOOD **SPACE**

Biographies

Luke Brady Jesus

Theatre includes: *The Fantasticks* (Duchess); *We Will Rock You, The Tempest* (Hurtwood House).

Opera includes: *Tarantula in Petrol Blue* (Snape Maltings Concert Hall).

Clare Burt Mom

Theatre includes: *Coram Boy, The Miracle, Sunday in the Park with George* (National); *Into the Woods, Nine, Company* (Donmar Warehouse); *Now You Know* (Metropolitan Room, NY); *Broken Glass,* (West Yorkshire Playhouse); *Cat on a Hot Tin Roof* (Dundee Rep); *Separate Tables, Harlequinade* (King's Head).

Television includes: *Criminal Justice, Woman of Substance.*

Film includes: *Intimacy, The Christmas Miracle, The Dance of Shiva.*

Daniel Cerqueira Lasalle/Dr Goosens/Pelayo

Theatre includes: *Joe Turner's Come and Gone, Some Voices, Amazônia, Afore Night Come* (Young Vic); *Sleeping Beauty* (Young Vic/Barbican/New Victory, NY); *Attempts on Her Life, Cleansed, Plasticine* (Royal Court); *The Girl on the Sofa* (Schaubühne am Lehninerplatz); *Arabian Nights* (RSC).

Film and television include: *The Woman in Black* (Hammer Films); *Rock & Chips, Spooks, Waking the Dead* (BBC); *Saving Private Ryan* (Dreamworks SKG).

Peter De Jersey Lally

Theatre includes: *House of Games* (Almeida); *Cat on a Hot Tin Roof* (Novello); *Troilus and Cressida, Darker Face of Earth, The Merchant of Venice, War and Peace* (National); *Hamlet* (Cheek by Jowl); *The Illusion* (Royal Exchange); *A Midsummer Night's Dream, Believe What You Will, Sejanus, Hamlet, As You Like It* (RSC).

Television includes: *Instinct, Sugar Rush II, Holby City, New Tricks.*

Film includes: *Out of Depth, The Bank Job.*

Joseph Drake Vernon

Joseph trained at the Bristol Old Vic Theatre School. *Vernon God Little* is his professional debut.

Credits while training include: Jason in *Pornography*, Pinchwife in *The Country Wife* and Hale in *The Crucible*.

Johnnie Fiori Pam

Theatre includes: *Hairspray, Thoroughly Modern Millie, 125th Street* (Shaftesbury); *Ma Rainey's Black Bottom* (Royal Exchange); *The Exonerated* (Riverside Studios); *The Wiz* (Hackney Empire).

Opera includes: *1984* (Royal Opera House).

Television includes: *Tinga Tinga Tales* (Tiger Aspect/Disney); *Chuggington* (Ludorum/Disney); *Teletubbies* (Ragdoll); *Living with the Dead* (Original); *Most Haunted* (Antix).

Lily James Ella/Taylor

Lily trained at the Guildhall School of Music and Drama.

Theatre includes: *The Last Five Years* (Barbican Pit).

Television includes: *Secret Diary of a Call Girl* (ITV); *Just William* (BBC).

Penny Layden Vaine/Leona/Team Leader

Theatre includes: *Romeo and Juliet, Helen* (Shakespeare's Globe); *The Spanish Tragedy* (Arcola); *Assassins* (Sheffield Crucible); *The Bacchae, Electra* (Royal Exchange); *The Tempest* (RSC); *Jane Eyre, A Passage to India* (Shared Experience); *Lidless* (Edinburgh/HighTide).

Television includes: *South Riding, Silent Witness* (BBC); *Poppy Shakespeare* (Channel 4 Films).

Film includes: *The Libertine* (Stanley Productions).

Nathan Osgood Sheriff Porkorney

Theatre includes: *Cradle Will Rock* (Arcola); *Aunt Dan and Lemon* (Royal Court); *Joan Rivers: A Work in Progress by a Life in Progress* (Leicester Square); *The Exonerated* (Dublin Festival); *Gem of the Ocean* (Tricycle); *His Girl Friday, Srebenica, Wind in the Willows* (National); *The Odd Couple* (Manchester Library); *Small Craft Warnings* (Pleasance).

Television includes: *The Shadow Line, Dalziel and Pascoe* (BBC).

Film includes: *Me and Orson Welles* (Dir: Richard Linklater); *Sahara* (Dir: Breck Eisner); *Mission Impossible* (Dir: Brian De Palma).

Nathan has also worked extensively in radio.

Duncan Wisbey Abdini and Show MD

Theatre includes: *Sleeping Beauty* (Young Vic/Broadway); *Hergé's Adventures of Tintin* (Young Vic/Barbican); *The Count of Monte Christo* (West Yorkshire Playhouse); *The Picture* (Salisbury Playhouse); *The Making of Moo* (Orange Tree, Richmond); *Dirty Fan Male* (Edinburgh Fringe/Bethnal Green Working Men's Club).

Television includes: *The Hive* (CITV); *The Big Impression, The Impressions Show* (BBC); *Pinky and Perky* (CBBC); *The Bill* (ITV); *No Signal* (FX).

Radio includes: *The Secret World, Laurence & Gus* (Radio 4); *News Jack* (BBC7).

Rufus Norris Director

Recent productions include *The Country Girl* in the West End, *Don Giovanni* at the ENO, *Death and the King's Horseman* at the National Theatre and the Broadway production of *Les Liaisons Dangereuses*.

Other London productions include *Cabaret, Festen* and *Tintin* in the West End; *Vernon God Little, Peribanez, Sleeping Beauty* and *Afore Night Come* (Young Vic); *Blood Wedding* (Almeida); *Market Boy* (National); *Under the Blue Sky* (Royal Court) and many others.

Alongside nominations for Olivier and Tony Awards, he has received two Evening Standard Awards (*Afore Night Come* and *Festen*), a Critics' Circle Award (*Festen*), and an Arts Foundation Fellowship.

Ian MacNeil Design

Theatre includes: *Afore Night Come, Peribanez* (Young Vic); *Festen* (Almeida/West End/Broadway); *An Inspector Calls* (National/world tour); *Machinal* (National); *Plasticine, A Number* (Royal Court); *Far Away* (Royal Court/West End/Broadway); *Billy Elliot* (West End/Broadway).

Nicky Gillibrand Costume

Nicky trained as a fashion textile designer. She works mostly as a costume designer in both theatre and opera and occasionally as a set designer. She was the winner of the Gold Award for Best Costume Design, Prague Quadrenale, 2003, for *A Midsummer Night's Dream,* Royal Shakespeare Theatre, director Richard Jones.

Theatre includes: *Annie Get Your Gun, The Good Soul of Szechuan, Six Characters in Search of an Author* (Young Vic); *King Lear* (Liverpool Playhouse/Young Vic); *The Tempest* (RSC); *The Seagull, Jumpers* (National); *Powerbook* (National/Paris/Rome); *Billy Elliot* (West End); *Camille* (set and costumes; Lyric Hammersmith).

Opera includes: *Lady Macbeth of Mtsensk, The Gambler* (Royal Opera House); *Peter Grimes* (ENO); *Don Giovanni* (Glyndebourne).

Film includes: *Institute Benjamenta* (directed by Brothers Quay).

Phil Bateman Musical Direction and Arrangement

Phil has just worked as MD/Arranger on *My Dad's a Birdman* at the Young Vic and *The Human Comedy* at the Young Vic/Watford Palace. He has been MD on three Olivier Award-winning shows: *Billy Elliot, Our House* and *Hello, Dolly!*

Theatre includes: As Musical Supervisor/Vocal Arranger: *Our House* (Cambridge Theatre/UK tour); *Imagine This* (New London/Plymouth and co-producer on cast recording). As Musical Director: *Billy Elliot* (Victoria Palace; original MD of show and cast album); *Hello, Dolly!, Gigi* (Regent's Park Open Air); *Treasure Island* (Rose, Kingston); *Piaf* (Sheffield Crucible); *Rodgers and Hammerstein's Cinderella* (Bristol Old Vic); *Return to the Forbidden Planet* (UK tour); *Wild, Wild Women* (Orange Tree, Richmond); *Cabaret* (Watermill); *Bridget Jones the Musical* (workshop).

Film includes: As Vocal Coach: *Kinky Boots, Cemetery Junction.*

Television includes: As Composer: *The Big Performance* (CBBC); *Body Story* (Channel 4).

Paule Constable Light

Theatre includes: *The Good Soul of Szechuan, generations* (Young Vic); *War Horse, Death and the King's Horseman, Phaedre* (National); *Oliver!, Love Never Dies* (West End); *Blasted* (Lyric Hammersmith); *Clybourne Park* (Royal Court); *Ivanov* (Donmar at the Wyndham's); *Les Misérables 25th Anniversary Production* (Barbican, international tour).

Opera includes: *Billy Budd* (Glyndebourne Festival); *Satyagraha* (ENO).

Dance includes: *Dorian Gray* (Matthew Bourne and New Adventures); *Goldberg Variations Project* with Tamara Rojo and Kim Branstrup (ROH2).

Jane Dutton Light

As relighter/programmer:

Theatre includes: *Tintin* (Young Vic/Barbican/West End); *Blasted, Watership Down* (Lyric Hammersmith); *The Gods Weep, Days of Significance* (RSC); *Don John* (Kneehigh/RSC); *Nights at the Circus* (Kneehigh/Lyric Hammersmith/UK tour); *The Man Who Had All the Luck* (Donmar Warehouse/UK tour); *Twelfth Night* (Donmar Warehouse/West End); *A Disappearing Number* (Complicite/ international tour); *Les Misérables 25th Anniversary Production* (Barbican, international tour).

Opera includes: *The Enchanted Pig* (Young Vic/The Opera Group); *Death in Venice* (Canadian Opera Company); *Five seasons of Garsington Opera, 2006–2010* (Garsington Opera Company).

Dance includes: *Dorian Gray* (Matthew Bourne and New Adventures).

Rich Walsh Sound

Theatre includes: *Strike Gently Away from Body* (Young Vic); *Under the Blue Sky* (Royal Court); *Welcome to Thebes, The Observer, The Five Wives of Maurice Pinder, The Alchemist, Primo* (National); *Von Ribbentrop's Watch* (Oxford Playhouse); *Dinner* (Wyndham's); *Fimbles Live!* (UK tour); *How to Be an Other Woman* (Gate); *Eigengrau* (Bush); *Small Craft Warnings* (Pleasance). As Associate Sound Designer: *Beauty and the Beast, The Cat in the Hat* (National).

Lizzi Gee Choreography

Theatre includes: *Love Story, Onassis, Daddy Cool* (West End); *Billy Elliot* (Victoria Palace; Resident Choreographer); *Buddy* (UK tour); all-male *Pirates of Penzance* (Union/Wilton's/Rose Kingston); *Sunshine on Leith* (Dundee Rep/UK tour); *Oliver!, The Sound of Music* (Larnala, Cyprus); *Hair* (Frankfurt English Speaking); *Snoopy* (New Players); *Silk workshop* (Orange Tree).

Television includes: *Legend of Dick and Dom; The Big Performance* with Gareth Malone (CBBC); *Feelgood Factor* (ITV); *Children's BAFTAs.*

Maggie Lunn Casting

Theatre includes: *Skellig* (Young Vic); *The Bridge Project* (Old Vic/BAM); *A Moon for the Misbegotten, Hamlet, Richard II* (Old Vic); *Cabaret* (West End); *Festen, Lady from the Sea* (Almeida).

Television includes: *Cranford* (I & II); *Nativity* (BBC).

Film includes: *Notes on a Scandal.*

Michaela Kennen Dialect

Theatre includes: *The Glass Menagerie* (Young Vic); *Eurydice, The Brothers Size* (Young Vic/ATC); *The Country Girl, Love Never Dies, Cabaret, Hairspray* (*West End*); *Jesus Hopped the 'A' Train* (Trafalgar Studios); *Songs from a Hotel Bedroom* (ROH Linbury); *The History Boys, The Rose Tattoo, Thérèse Raquin, Caroline, or Change, Market Boy, Playing with Fire* (National).

Rikki Henry Assistant Direction

Rikki graduated from UCA with a degree in Film Production in 2009.

Directing credits include: *Project Underworld* (Bristol Old Vic/ATC); *Woza Albert!* (Stonecrabs Theatre Young Director Programme); *The Moment Before* (The Warehouse Theatre as part of the Strawberry Picking Festival).

Assistant directing credits include: *Annie Get Your Gun* (Young Vic); *Ghosts or Those Who Return* (Arcola).

Rikki is Jerwood Assistant Director.

DBC Pierre

DBC Pierre lives in County Leitrim, Ireland.

Vernon God Little, his debut novel, won the Man Booker Prize and the Whitbread First Novel Award and the PG Wodehouse Award for Comic Fiction.

Ludmila's Broken English was published in 2006 and *Lights Out in Wonderland* was published in 2010.

DBC Pierre's books are published in over forty languages.

Tanya Ronder

Stage adaptations include *Peribanez* (Lope de Vega), Young Vic and Company B, Australia; *Blood Wedding* (Lorca), Almeida; *Night Flight* (Saint Exupéry) Muztheater, Amsterdam; *Macbett* (Ionesco) RSC; *Filumena* (de Filippo), Almeida, scheduled 2011; *Peter Pan* (JM Barrie) in a 1200-seat tent in Kensington Gardens, O2 and San Francisco with a continuing USA tour and a new tent opening in New Zealand.

Film includes *King Bastard*, (UK Film Council/BBC, starring Peter Mullan); *Random*, (UKFC, Little Bird), in development.

Also in development is *The Table,* a project with Rufus Norris, developed with the support of RNT Studio and *Liolá* (Pirandello) commissioned by the National in 2011.

The Young Vic

'Thank God for the Young Vic'
The Observer

'One of Britain's most consistently imaginative theatres'
The Daily Telegraph

Our shows
We present the widest variety of classics, new plays, forgotten works and music theatre. We tour and co-produce extensively within the UK and internationally.

Our artists
Our shows are created by some of the world's great theatre people alongside the most adventurous of the younger generation. This fusion makes the Young Vic one of the most exciting theatres in the world.

Our audience
...is famously the youngest and most diverse in London. We encourage those who don't think theatre is 'for them' to make it part of their lives. We give 10% of our tickets to schools and neighbours irrespective of box-office demand, and keep prices low.

Our partners near at hand
Each year we engage with 10,000 local people – individuals and groups of all kinds including schools and colleges – by exploring theatre on and off stage. From time to time we invite our neighbours to appear on our stage alongside professionals.

Our partners further away
By co-producing with leading theatre, opera, and dance companies from around the world we challenge ourselves and create shows neither partner could achieve alone.

The Young Vic is a company limited by guarantee, registered in England No. 1188209 VAT Registration No. 236 673 348 The Young Vic (registered charity no. 268876) receives public funding from:

Supporting the Young Vic

The Young Vic relies on the generous support of many trusts, companies and individuals to continue our work, on and off stage. For their recent support we thank

Public Funders
Arts Council England
Lambeth Borough Council
London Development Agency
Southwark Council

Corporate Supporters
American Airlines
Barclays Capital
Bloomberg
Bupa
De La Rue Charitable Trust
HSBC Bank plc
KPMG Foundation
Lane Consulting
Markit
The Merlin Entertainment
London Eye
Shell

Big Cheese Corporate Members
Bloomberg
Cantor Fitzgerald
HgCapital
Ingenious Media Plc
Land Securities
Sense Worldwide

Hot Shot Corporate Members
Clifford Chance
Slaughter and May
Taylor Wessing LLP

Trust Supporters
The City Bridge Trust
Fund of the Capital
 Community Foundation
 Dorset Foundation
Clore Duffield Foundation
The Drapers' Company
D'Oyly Carte Charitable Trust
Equitable Charitable Trust
Eranda Foundation
Ernest Cook Trust
Esmée Fairbairn Foundation
Foundation for Sport
 & the Arts

Garfield Weston Foundation
Garrick Charitable Trust
Genesis Foundation
The Golden Bottle Trust
Goethe-Institut
Goldsmiths' Company
Gosling Foundation
Help a London Child
Henry Smith Charity
Jerwood Charitable
 Foundation
John Ellerman Foundation
John Thaw Foundation
The Limbourne Trust
Man Group plc Charitable
 Trust
Martin Bowley Charitable
 Trust
Medicor Foundation
Peter Minet Trust
The Progress Foundation
The Royal Victoria Hall
 Foundation
Trust for London
Steel Charitable Trust
Quercus Trust
The Worshipful Company of
 Grocers
29th May 1961
Charitable Trust

Production Partnership
Tony & Gisela Bloom
Sandy Chalmers
Kay Ellen Consolver
 & John Storkerson
Mr & Mrs Roderick Jack
Chris & Jane Lucas
Miles Morland
Nadine Majaro
 & Roger Pilgrim
Anda & Bill Winters

Best Friends
Jane Attias
Chris & Frances Bates
Anthony & Karen Beare
The Bickertons
Katie Bradford
Jennifer & Jeff Eldredge
Sarah Hall
Richard Hardman & Family
Nik Holttum
 & Helen Brannigan
Suzanne & Michael Johnson
Tom Keatinge
John Kinder
 & Gerry Downey
Carol Lake
Simon & Midge Palley
Naomi Russell
Charles & Donna Scott
Justin Shinebourne
The Tracy Family
Leo & Susan van der Linden
Rob Wallace
Andrew Wylde

Great Friends
Angus Aynsley
 & Miel de Botton Aynsley
Tim & Caroline Clark
Robyn Durie
Susan Hyland
Stephen & Angela Jordan
Ann Lewis
Tony Mackintosh
Ian McKellen
Barbara Minto
Georgia Oetker
Jon & Noralee Sedmak
Bhagat Sharma
Donna & Richard Vinter
Jimmy & Carol Walker

The Young Vic Ruby Partners

To mark the 40th year of the Young Vic, the following companies have generously partnered with us. Their gifts will make a contribution to our work on stage as well as to the thousands of opportunities we offer each year to local schools, colleges and neighbours to discover themselves through theatre.

 BARCLAYS CAPITAL

Bloomberg

INGENIΘUS MEDIA

 lane

TaylorWessing

 THE CUT
BAR | RESTAURANT | CAFÉ

 BANCROFT WINES

 Jones
Furniture and Catering Equipment

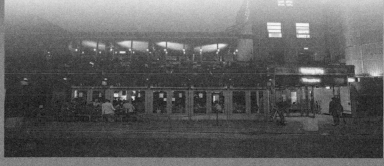

Young Vic Ruby Partners have supported us through the Forever Young 40th Anniversary Fundraising campaign.

FOREVER YOUNG

The Young Vic (registered charity no. 268876)

Taylor Wessing
is proud to sponsor the
Young Vic

TaylorWessing

www.taylorwessing.com

Berlin Brussels Cambridge Dubai Düsseldorf Frankfurt Hamburg London Munich Paris Beijing◻ Shanghai◻ Warsaw△

◻Representative offices   △Associated office

TAKE YOUR SEATS.

American Airlines is the official airline partner
of the Young Vic Theatre.

 AmericanAirlines®

AA.com

VERNON GOD LITTLE

Adapted for the stage by Tanya Ronder

From the book by DBC Pierre

Note

Unfortunately, most of the songs in the script cannot be detailed in full because of copyright restrictions. However, they do form an integral part of the play, splicing between the lines of dialogue as indicated.

The music could be different in another production – both the choice of songs and who plays or sings what – but the inclusion of music throughout, the underscoring of the action and the feathering of sung lines with dialogue, is a vital element in the escalating speed and energy of the story.

The 2011 production featured ten actors (see page 102 for details of doubling). This number could be expanded (or possibly reduced) in future productions. The assignment of roles could also be different, including the gender of many of the characters.

A forward slash in the text (/) marks the point where the next character begins to speak.

4

Characters

VERNON
JESUS
VAINE
SHERIFF PORKORNEY
PAM
EILEENA
MOM
LALLY
LEONA
BRAD
MR ABDINI
COURT OFFICER
JUDGE HELEN GURIE
DR GOOSENS
TAYLOR FIGUEROA
PASTOR GIBBONS
KID IN BRACES
MR KEETER
ELLA KEETER
TEAM LEADER
STEVEN
TODD
MAY-MAY

HEAVY
LALLY'S MOM
SILAS
MR DEUTSCHMAN
BUS DRIVER
LITTLE OLD LADY
CHRISSIE
BORDER GUARD
BARTENDER
PELAYO
PELAYO'S WIFE
ACAPULCO CLERK
CAMERAMAN
BRIAN
PROSECUTOR
JUDGE
MEDIA COURT OFFICER
FOREMAN
JONESY
CON ONE
CON TWO
LASALLE

Also bus passengers, camera crew, convicts, singers, teenagers, etc.

This text went to press before the end of rehearsals and so may differ slightly from the play as performed.

PRE-SHOW

MR KEETER *sings a short number with his guitar to both settle and unsettle the audience.*

ACT ONE

VERNON *sits in the interview room. In his memory, school mates shout abuse, 'Meskin Bambi boy', etc. There are gunshots.* JESUS *sings 'Crazy' by Patsy Cline.*

VAINE. Vernon Gregory Little?

    VERNON *shares the joke with* JESUS.

VERNON. No, it's Dolly fucken Parton.

VAINE. What?

    JESUS *stops singing.*

VERNON. Sorry.

VAINE. Your habitual place of residence is 17 Beulah Drive?

VERNON. Yes, ma'am.

VAINE. Who else resides there?

VERNON. Just my mom.

VAINE. And you're fifteen years old?

VERNON. Nearly sixteen.

VAINE. Awkward age.

VERNON. Ma'am, will this take long?

VAINE. Vernon, we're talking accessory to murder here, it'll take as long as it takes.

VERNON. But –

VAINE. Don't tell me you weren't Jesus Navarro's only friend, don't you tell me that for one second.

JESUS *slinks off*.

VERNON. No, ma'am, but... Ask Lori Donner, she knows I wasn't there!

VAINE. You were found at the scene of the massacre with a bag of ammunition in your arms, are you with me, Mr Little?

He looks at her.

Can you account for yourself at a quarter after ten, Tuesday morning?

VERNON. I was in school.

VAINE. What period?

VERNON. Math.

VAINE. Math?

VERNON. Ma'am, I didn't see it happen, I was – behind the gym.

VAINE. You take math behind the gym?

VERNON. No, it was our math period...

VAINE. Why weren't you in class?

VERNON. I went to the bathroom.

VAINE. Behind the gym?

VERNON. I wasn't there, ma'am, I have witnesses.

VAINE. Is that right?

VERNON. Ask Mr Nuckles!

VAINE. Mr Nuckles and who else?

VERNON. A whole bunch of people.

VAINE. Where are those people now?

VERNON *smarts*.

Exactly. Not the most reliable witnesses in their body bags, are they, Vernon? Let me ask you two simple questions: one – are you involved with drugs?

VERNON. No.

VAINE. Two – do you possess a firearm?

SHERIFF PORKORNEY *joins them*.

SHERIFF PORKORNEY. There's a lot of bothered folk outside, son.

VERNON. I wasn't in the room, sir...

SHERIFF PORKORNEY. You were friendly though, huh, with the crazy Meskin boy?

VERNON. Sir, I never dreamed he would...

SHERIFF PORKORNEY. Yeah? (*To* VAINE.) Examine Little's clothes, did you?

VAINE. Yes, sir.

SHERIFF PORKORNEY. Undergarments?

VAINE. Regular Y-fronts.

SHERIFF PORKORNEY. Check the back of 'em, did you, Vaine? Certain type of practices can loosen a man's pitoota.

VAINE. Seemed clean, Sheriff.

VERNON. Sir, I ain't gay, you could just ask.

SHERIFF PORKORNEY. Regular boy then, are you, son? Like your cars and your girls?

VERNON. Yes, sir.

SHERIFF PORKORNEY. And your guns?

No answer.

All right, let's see if it's true. How many offices does a girl have that you can get more'n one finger into?

VERNON. Offices?

SHERIFF PORKORNEY. Cavities, holes.

VERNON. Uh... two?

SHERIFF PORKORNEY. Wrong, what a surprise. Vaine, get your paperwork, hold the boy.

They leave. JESUS *is back.*

VERNON (*to* JESUS). Pitoota? Fucken retard. 'Are you with me, Mr Little?' No, I'm at the mall dicking your fucken daughters!

PAM (*in her Mercury*). Eileena, have you seen Vern, has he been fed?

VERNON. Pam?

EILEENA. You better wait outside, Pam...

PAM *drives right up to* VERNON *in her car.*

PAM. Your mom's baking so I've come to fetch you. You eaten today?

VERNON. No.

PAM. Oh, Lord! I got us some chicken mix.

EILEENA. You can't take him, Pam –

PAM. Eileena, you tell the Sheriff this boy ain't eaten. (*To* VERNON.) Hop in.

EILEENA. Vaine's filling out the papers!

VERNON. I better stay, Pam.

PAM. Malarkey, come on now.

EILEENA. They're holding him, Pam…

PAM. Love your hair.

EILEENA. Not too frisky?

PAM. Lord, no, it suits you. Jump in, Vern.

He can't resist.

EILEENA. Sheriff!

'Galveston' by Jimmy Webb, sung by Glen Campbell, plays on the car stereo.

PAM. Eat up, you must be starvin'.

VERNON. Mom okay?

PAM. Well, she spent her last dime on cake mix for the grievin' families.

(*Singing along with the tape.*) Galveston, oh, Galveston… I still hear your sea winds blowing…

Eat the bottom pieces before they get soggy.

(*Singing.*) I still see her dark eyes glowing… She was twenty-one…

Sing with me, Vern!

(*Singing.*) When I left Galveston.

Come on, Vernie, whatever happens we still need to sing!

PAM *and* VERNON (*singing*). Galveston, oh Galveston…

VAINE. Stop that car!

PAM. Sixteen soon, little Vern!

DRIVER. Move your ass, road hog.

VAINE *pursues* PAM*'s Mercury in her police car.* EILEENA, SHERIFF PORKORNEY, VAINE *and the* COMPANY *join in singing. They hit the Martirio Highway.*

PAM, VERNON *and* COMPANY (*singing*).
  I still hear your sea waves crashin'...

PAM (*singing*). Crash, crash, crash...

PAM, VERNON *and* COMPANY (*singing*).
  While I watch the cannons flashin'...

PAM *and* VERNON (*singing*).
  Flash, flash, flash...

PAM, VERNON *and* COMPANY (*singing*).
  I clean my gun, and dream of Galveston.

  MOM *is stuffing cakes into her mouth to quell her tension.
  The music stops.*

VERNON. Hi, Mom.

MOM. Vern, hi! Joy cake?

  VAINE *catches them up in her police car.*

  Vaine, just in time for cake!

VAINE (*climbing from her car*). Your son absconded from our
  interview.

MOM. Nabscunded? (*Offering the cakes.*) Fresh from the stove,
  help yourself.

VAINE. No, Mrs Little, I have to get your son back to the
  station, then we'll need to take a look through his room.

VERNON. My room?

MOM. Why, Vaine? Everybody knows who caused the tragedy...

VAINE. We know the effect of the tragedy, Mrs Little, we'll see
  about the cause. Vernon, get in the car.

MOM. Why does everything happen to me? He says he wasn't
  in class!

VAINE. Where was he, then, behind the gym? Suspects with
  airtight alibis don't abscond from interviews!

PAM. I took him, Vaine, he was near dead from starvation!

VAINE. I'm takin' the child back...

MOM. Wait! There's something you should know. Stress brings on his condition.

VERNON. Momma!

MOM. Vernon Gregory, you know you get that inconvenience!

VERNON. Mom, please...

PAM. Doris...

MOM. He's kind of unpredictable for Number Twos...

VERNON. Jesus fuck.

VAINE (*dragging him off*). I'll keep the Sheriff informed.

MOM. Take some spares, it's a clinical condition!

    LALLY *appears, heroically, with a camcorder.*

LALLY (*to* VAINE). Captain?

MOM, PAM *and* VAINE (*gasping*). Huh?

LALLY. A few words for the camera?

VAINE. Firstly, sir, I'm a deputy, and secondly, reporters should consult the media room for updates.

LALLY. Actually, I'm doing a background story.

VAINE (*clears her throat*). Gghrr.

LALLY. Eulalio Ledesma, ma'am, at your service. (*He downs the liquid from a small bottle*.) The world awaits.

VAINE. The world's a long way from Martirio, Mr Ledes-ghmm...

LALLY. Today, ma'am, the world is Martirio.

PAM. TV, Vaine!

VAINE. I can't go on like this, I'm not prepared…

PAM. Poohf, you're spotless.

VAINE. What am I s'posed to say?

PAM. Get a grip, Vaine, wanna shuffle papers for ever?

LALLY. Relax, I'll lead you right in. Hit it, boys.

> *The gathering crowd plays Mariachi-type news music.*
> LALLY *points the camera at himself.*

> Once again, America dons the cloak of mourning. Sixteen young lives laid to waste on what should have been just another innocent day in the small town of Martirio, central Texas. Now we ask, how do we heal these wounds? We begin on the front line with our law-enforcement professionals. (*Swinging the camera onto* VAINE, *sotto voce.*) The camera'll love you…

> Deputy Vaine Gurie, does the community relate differently to you at a time like this?

VAINE. This is the first time we've had a high-school massacre in Martirio.

LALLY. And is the community pulling together?

VAINE. We have back-up officers over from Luling and, uh, Ryesburg sent us some home-made fudge…

LALLY. The extra officers free you up to spend time with survivors?

VAINE. Sir, the survivors have survived. (*Warming to her theme.*) I'm lookin' to find the cause.

LALLY. It's not open and shut?

VAINE. That's a lot of carnage for one, unaided gunman to manage.

LALLY (*grabbing* VERNON). Did this young man cause it?

VAINE (*losing confidence*). That's not what I said…

LALLY. Then why should the American taxpayer bankroll you to detain him?

PAM (*to* MOM *and* VERNON). Do you think Sheriff knows Vaine's on TV?

VAINE. That'll be all for now, Mr Lesama. (*Re: the news-music.*) Quit that noise.

LALLY. Deputy, this is the public domain... Boys!

The music resumes.

PAM (*on phone*). Eileena? Vaine's on TV...

VAINE. Put the camera away now, Mr Lesama.

LALLY. God Himself can't stop it rollin', Deputy.

Her phone goes.

I think that's your phone.

VAINE (*answering*). Sheriff? Back to the office? Right away, sir.

She scuttles off, leaving VERNON.

LALLY (*to the mariachi band*). Wrap it, boys.

PAM. See you later, little Vern!

LALLY. Guess that's the Deputy off your back, kid!

PAM (*pursuing her in the car*). NYPD Blues next, Vaine...

MOM. Oh, Mr Smedma...

LALLY. Eulalio Ledesma, ma'am. Educated people call me Lally.

MOM. I'm Doris. Can I get you a Coke, Lally, to thank you?

LALLY. Just water for me, and maybe one of those beautiful cakes.

MOM. Joy cakes. Help yourself!

LALLY. Thank you, they look joyful.

MOM. Come on inside. (*Handing* VERNON *the cakes*.)
Vernon! So, Lally, do you stay nearby, or…?

LALLY. In the van, right now. With all the media interest,
motels are mobbed…

MOM. Oh.

LALLY. I heard some generous townsfolk are taking in guests,
but I've not been fortunate yet.

MOM. Well, I…

The loud burst of an Eldorado horn interrupts them.

LEONA. Hi, Doris!

VERNON. Shit-sniffers.

MOM. Vernon! Hi, guys, this is Mr Lesama, from the TV.

LEONA. Hi, I'm Leona, this is my son Bradley, I had him
young, say hi, Bradley.

LALLY. Hi, Brad.

VERNON. What's that smell?

BRAD. Pluck off.

LEONA. Bradley Pritchard!

BRAD. Goddam what? I said 'pluck' for chrissakes, I mean,
shit!

He smacks his mother, she smacks him back, a fight erupts.

LEONA. Bradley! (*Cool again.*) So, Vaine was here again?
What does she want with Vernon?

MOM. I don't know why she's picking on him…

LEONA. Well, he was friends with that scary psycho Meskin
boy.

LALLY. Crazy, huh?

LEONA. Did you know the Meskin was wearing silk panties when he killed them?

BRAD (*to* VERNON). You wear girls' panties too?

VERNON. Fuck you, dork hole.

LALLY *opens up another small bottle to drink.*

BRAD. What's he drinking?

VERNON. Piss.

LALLY. Siberian Ginseng Compound for men. (*Throwing one to* VERNON.) Here, son, use it when you need it, know what I'm saying? Better than Viagra!

LEONA. Really? (*Giggling.*) Hmn, hmn, hmn, hmn…

LALLY *winks at* MOM.

MOM. I'll get your water. You coming, Leona?

LALLY. Need a hand?

MOM. No, no, you relax. It's nice for Vernon to have a man to talk to.

LALLY. No father, huh, Doris?

MOM. Not any more. He passed away three years ago now, though you'd never guess it, I'm still waiting on the insurance!

LEONA. Honey, they can't pay out before they have a body, you know that!

MOM. That's right, a body. (*Ushering* LEONA *off, laughing nervously.*) Anyway, anyway…

LEONA. Bradley!

He follows.

LALLY. Vern, you're innocent, right?

VERNON. Yeah.

LALLY. You should tell your story, big man, clear your name. I'd be prepared to help.

VERNON. You already did.

LALLY. Camera wasn't running.

VERNON. No?

LALLY. Call it a favour between underdogs.

VERNON. Underdogs?

LALLY. You need to speak out.

VERNON. But, like, I didn't do anything.

LALLY. Excuse my language, son, but, who fucking cares? People decide with or without the facts. If you don't get out there and paint your paradigm, someone else'll paint it for you.

VERNON. My what?

LALLY. You never heard of the paradigm shift? Example, you see a man with his hand up your granny's ass, what do you think?

VERNON. Bastard!

LALLY. Then you learn a deadly bug crawled up there and the man has, in fact, put aside his disgust to save Granny – what do you think now?

VERNON. Hero.

LALLY. *Voilà*, a paradigm shift. The data doesn't change, the information you use to judge it, does. You were ready to crucify the guy, now you want to shake his hand.

VERNON. I don't think so…

LALLY. Huurr, you're smart. You need positioning, Vern, like a new product on the market.

VERNON. But I have witnesses.

LALLY. No problem, then. They can illuminate why you were found with the gunman's bag of ammunition...

VERNON. I just found his bag on the floor...

LALLY. Sure. And I'm guessing you're clean, too? Coz they're hot on this drugs idea.

VERNON. Drugs?

LALLY. They're asking how anyone not on drugs could orchestrate such a rampage. Which is why they've brought in the dogs.

VERNON. Dogs?

LALLY. To sniff out the naughties. But if you're clean, there's nothing to worry about when they search your room, is there?

Dogs bark, VERNON *hits his room.* JESUS *is there, plucking his guitar, the intro to 'Rhinestone Cowboy' by Larry Weiss.*

VERNON. Drugs, my ball sack! Since when did we have the fucken money for drugs, duh? You flip out and suddenly I'm a criminal? Shit. (*Finding it.*) One precious joint you stole from your pop... what am I supposed to do with this? (*He puts it behind his ear. He finds something else, reads the label.*) LSD? Aw hell, no, Taylor's drugs, shit, shit, shit! Okay, it's okay, Vern, think, think clearly, they're gonna search your room with dogs. I mean, what kind of fucken life is this? Come on, help me, man, where can I hide it...?

JESUS *is no use.* VERNON *comes across the bottle.*

In Lally's piss!

(*Singing a rap while putting the gels in* LALLY*'s bottle.*)
So what we be thinkin' of this,
The drugs laid low in the piss,
I got away from the 5.0,

Escaped from the guy,
Pam got the whip and got started,
I'm fly,
I'm on a rollercoaster, casino poker,
Search my room and you'll look like a joker,
TV man threw me tips on the sofa,
Now I'm living la vida loca!

(*Imitating* BRAD.) 'You wear girls' panties too?' (*Picking it up*.) Oooooh, Mom's underwear catalogue – Lingerie squad, freeze, it's a panty-cult, string him up! Hurgh. Oops.

Some pages drop out. BRAD*'s foot lands on them.* JESUS *has gone.*

BRAD. Amputee pornography, huh? Cool. (*Keeping the pages*.) Your mom wants you.

VERNON. Shame your mom never wanted you!

BRAD (*re: his own shoes*). Air Max's, new, two hundred dollars.

VERNON (*re: his shoes*). Jordan New Jacks, priceless.

BRAD. Twenty dollars. (*Re: his own*.) Two hundred.

VERNON. Eat shit, Brad Prat-chard.

MOM. Vernon?

VERNON. Yeah?

MOM. Run downstairs and ask that nice TV man if he'd like to stay a couple of nights.

VERNON. Do what?

MOM. There's no room at any of the motels… Go!

VERNON *finds* LALLY. *'Rhinestone Cowboy' intro is up to speed now.*

VERNON. Mr Ledesma?

LALLY. Big man!

VERNON. My mom asked me to ask you if you'd like to stay at ours tonight.

LALLY. Your mom is a rare Christian, Vern.

Dogs bark, a siren whines.

(*Indicating his camera.*) We could give a new POV, Vern. True-life story of a regular boy…

VERNON. Yeah?

LALLY. Sure. We could talk to your mom, film your room…

LALLY *spots the joint, snatches it.*

Woo-hoo, you could've just said you didn't want to share!

VERNON. Uh, shit, it ain't mine actually…

The dogs and sirens encroach.

LALLY. No worries, I'm good at hiding things.

VERNON. I appreciate that, sir!

SHERIFF PORKORNEY. Vernon Gregory Little, I have a warrant for your arrest.

VERNON. Arrest? But I didn't even do anything!

LALLY. Camera's loaded, big man, leave it with me.

MOM. Sheriff, no, he has a clinical condition…!

LEONA. Hi, Sheriff.

LALLY *starts to sing 'Rhinestone Cowboy', interspersing each sung line between the lines of dialogue.*

SHERIFF PORKORNEY. Let's take a ride, son.

LALLY *sings.*

MOM. Sheriff was just passing…

LALLY *sings,* SHERIFF PORKORNEY *handcuffs* VERNON.

Actually, I thought it was my new refrigerator…

VERNON. They're arresting me, Mom...!

She doesn't hear him, she's busy making up lies.

MOM. Which I ordered weeks ago!

Everyone is now singing the backing to LALLY's *song.*

Special edition.

They sing.

Joy cake, anyone?

And sing.

Sheriff?

The song reaches its crescendo and stops. MOM *races after* VERNON *as he's driven away.*

Vernon, I love you! Even murderers are loved by their families, you know!

VERNON. Heck, Ma, I ain't a murderer!

MOM. Honey, I know, I'm just saying...

VERNON. Shit, Mr Ledesma, do your film, tell 'em the fucken truth!

Everybody sings the rousing final chorus of 'Rhinestone Cowboy'. Silence.

SHERIFF PORKORNEY (*in the police car*). You ain't pullin' your rod back there, are ya, Little? Porkin' the preacher, tossin' the ham javelin, rememberin' your Meskin boy? Get out, your attorney's here.

MR ABDINI. Hello, Bernon, how are you? My name is Abdini, I'm your tar-ney.

He's dressed in white, Turkish-disco style, and has an unintelligible accent.

VERNON. My torney?

MR ABDINI. Come, we have pearly-money herring.

VERNON. Pearly-money...?

MR ABDINI. Herring. (*Putting him in a chair.*) Make sit, Bernon. You touch bag, make fingerprince?

VERNON. Sorry?

MR ABDINI. Finger-prince, finger-prince on ammunition bag?

VERNON. Fingerprints? I guess so.

MR ABDINI. You tell me whappen.

VERNON. Excuse me?

MR ABDINI. Whappen in school.

VERNON. School? Well, I was out of class and –

MR ABDINI. Batroom, you went batroom?

VERNON. I went...? Yeah, but that wasn't...

MR ABDINI. Anyone else in batroom?

VERNON. Sorry? No, see, it wasn't actually in the bathroom...

MR ABDINI. You go batroom but not go batroom to go batroom? Ah! Pee-pees or poo-poos? Very impotent evidentse.

From court, interrupting MR ABDINI.

COURT OFFICER. Court-a-rise for Judge Helen Gurie...

MR ABDINI. Ssh, I fine out. You don tsetse-fly today, we try bail.

JUDGE HELEN GURIE. How long has this young man been in custody?

VAINE. We're trying to ascertain the boy's whereabouts, ma'am, at the time of the murders.

JUDGE HELEN GURIE. And?

VAINE. He was found with Jesus Navarro's ammunition bag in his arms, ma'am.

JUDGE HELEN GURIE. And?

VAINE. We hoped a particular piece of evidence would come in by now, ma'am.

JUDGE HELEN GURIE. You hoped it would come in?

VAINE. Yes, ma'am. We already searched the school for a second firearm. We may have to look further afield...

JUDGE HELEN GURIE. And why exactly are you looking for a second gun?

VAINE. In case the witness was intending to use it, Your Honour.

JUDGE HELEN GURIE. May I remind you that the child is not on trial here. You cannot detain him on a whim.

VAINE *clears her throat.*

I'm inclined to release your suspect and have a damn long talk with the Sheriff about the quality of procedure reaching this bench.

EILEENA. She ain't seen it yet.

COURT OFFICER. She ain't seen it yet.

EILEENA. She ain't seen it yet.

JUDGE HELEN GURIE. What is going on here? Has this court slipped into a parallel universe, have I been left behind?

VAINE. There's been a report, ma'am, about the suspect, on television...

JUDGE HELEN GURIE. Where's my remote?

LALLY*'s news music is more important-sounding, his television a little larger.*

LALLY (*on TV*). To his neighbours, Vernon Gregory Little seemed like a normal teenage boy who wouldn't attract attention walking any downtown street, until today.

(*Disordered xylophone music.*) Whilst the bereaved families of Martirio are preparing their young for burial we have to ask, why did Vernon befriend the outsider, Jesus Navarro? Is it normal for a boy to be a mass-murderer's buddy? Is it acceptable for a teenager to have a room full of pornography?

VERNON. Shit.

EILEENA (*re: LALLY*). He's cute!

LALLY (*on TV; re: the lingerie catalogue*). An innocent prop, or a chilling link to Tuesday's crimes?

He flips through the pages until the flipping stops.

JUDGE HELEN GURIE. What is that, where's my glasses?

COURT OFFICER. It's a lingerie catalogue, ma'am, with some pages stuck together.

JUDGE HELEN GURIE. Oh.

LALLY (*on TV*). As his mother, you maintain Vernon's innocence, right?

MOM (*on TV*). Oh God, a child is always innocent to his mother, I mean, even murderers are loved by their families, you know...

VERNON. Shit, Mom!

LALLY (*on TV*). Maybe Vernon Little's private library holds the key? No Steinbeck, no Hemingway – his literary tastes stretch only to this.

He holds up a page of amputee pornography.

VERNON. Thanks, Brad.

JUDGE. What is that?

EILEENA. Amputee pornography, that looks like the Horny Hoppers series 2010...

COURT OFFICER. Oh...

LALLY (*on TV*). I'm Eulalio Ledesma.

VERNON. Holy paradigm, man...

JUDGE HELEN GURIE (*switching off the TV*). Well. Well, well.

VERNON. Ma'am, this whole thing can be cleared up by my witnesses, my teacher, Mr Nuckles an' all...

JUDGE HELEN GURIE. Counsel, please inform your client that he's not on trial here. (*Quietly.*) Vaine, you have checked alibi witnesses?

VAINE. The last witness, Miss Lori Donner, passed away this morning, Judge.

VERNON. Lori? No, he wouldn't kill Lori...

VAINE. Making seventeen dead.

JUDGE HELEN GURIE. And the teacher?

VAINE. Mr Nuckles can't speak, from shock. The doctors say he may never speak again.

MR ABDINI. We apply bail, Your Honour.

JUDGE HELEN GURIE. I'm sorry?

VAINE. Judge, the boy has a history of absconding...

MR ABDINI. But little man is part family home, he's baby...

JUDGE HELEN GURIE. What did he say?

COURT OFFICER. I think he's applying for bail, Your Honour...

VAINE. It's a single-parent family, Judge...

JUDGE HELEN GURIE. Is the father contactable?

VAINE. No, ma'am, he's presumed deceased, although his body's never been found.

JUDGE HELEN GURIE. And the mother, she not in court today?

VAINE. She was awaiting delivery of a refrigerator.

JUDGE HELEN GURIE. Vernon Gregory Little, commensurate with my responsibility to this community, I am releasing you –

VAINE. Objection, your Honour!

JUDGE HELEN GURIE (*'Bam!' goes her hammer*). – into the daily, outpatient care –

VAINE. Your Honour –

JUDGE HELEN GURIE (*'Bam!'*). – with a non-negotiable schedule –

VAINE. But –

JUDGE HELEN GURIE. Of the psychiatrist, Dr Oliver Goosens! (*'Bam!'*)

Back at home.

VERNON. How could you do that to me, Ma?

MOM. I only told the truth, Vernon, and anyway, how could you do all this to me?

VERNON. I haven't done anything, print me a fucken T-shirt!

MOM. Don't you curse at me, young man!

VERNON. Never let Eulalio in this house again, okay?

MOM. Oh, Vernon, you just wouldn't understand. It's a woman's thing.

VERNON. I have to go to the psychiatrist's.

MOM. Wait! Vern? He might want to ask about your family and… it's best not to mention anything about your daddy's –

VERNON. Body?

MOM. No…

VERNON. No?

MOM. Yes! Well, and…

VERNON. Gun?

MOM. Probably best to keep it between ourselves.

VERNON. I know, Ma.

MOM. Mm. Don't forget to floss!

DR GOOSENS. Vernon Gregory, how are you today?

VERNON. Okay, I guess.

DR GOOSENS. Alrighty. And what can you tell me about why you're here?

VERNON. The Judge must think I'm crazy or something.

DR GOOSENS. And are you?

VERNON. I guess that ain't up to me to say.

DR GOOSENS. I'm here to help, Vernon. Please try to be candid. If you open yourself up to this process, you may even find it beneficial. Let's see if this helps.

He plays some gentle Holst.

Now, tell me, if you can, how do you feel about what's happened?

VERNON. Uh, wrecked.

DR GOOSENS. What is it making you feel that way?

VERNON. School.

DR GOOSENS. You mean, what happened at school that day?

VERNON. Yeah.

DR GOOSENS. You were Jesus's friend?

VERNON. Yeah.

DR GOOSENS. I understand he wasn't a popular kid?

VERNON. That's just coz no one knew him –

DR GOOSENS. Believe me, Jesus touched me too, his youth, his rage, the whole affair touched me deeply.

VERNON (*spilling*). Everybody knows Jesus caused the tragedy but they can't kill him for it because he already did that himself and now they're looking at me and calling me the psycho!

DR GOOSENS. Was he your only friend, Vernon?

VERNON. No.

DR GOOSENS. You have other friends?

VERNON. Not so many now. Lori Donner, the nicest girl in class times a zillion, died too.

DR GOOSENS. Any other girls?

VERNON. Uh, one. She'd quit school already.

DR GOOSENS. Okay.

VERNON. Taylor Figueroa.

DR GOOSENS. Someone with whom you had physical contact, perhaps?

VERNON. Kind of.

DR GOOSENS. You can tell me, Vernon. What do you remember about your contact with Taylor?

VERNON. Uh, her skin, I guess.

TAYLOR. Oh my God, I'm so wasted...

DR GOOSENS. Her skin?

TAYLOR. I need to lie down.

VERNON. The smell of her skin.

TAYLOR. Urh, thank you, in case I, like, pass out or whatever. Who are you?

VERNON. She smelled – warm.

TAYLOR. Vernon? Vern, can you, like, undo my shorts? Just peel 'em off, whatever, I'm so wasted I can't breathe. Oh God, that's good, that feels...

DR GOOSENS. And how did her warm skin make you feel?

TAYLOR. Vern, will you look after these for me? Nasty acid, nasty, nasty gels. I can't keep 'em, my parents'll kill me.

DR GOOSENS. Vernon?

TAYLOR. You're cute, kiss me.

DR GOOSENS. Vernon?

TAYLOR. Vernon, cutie…

DR GOOSENS. Alrighty, so, Vernon, tell me a bit about your friendship with Jesus.

VERNON. Jesus?

DR GOOSENS. How did you spend time together, how did you relax?

VERNON. We just – hung out.

DR GOOSENS. At home?

The music is working on VERNON.

VERNON. Mostly at, like, Keeter's, that wasteland at the edge of town.

DR GOOSENS (*making a note*). The Keeter's property?

VERNON. We had a den in this old quarry.

DR GOOSENS. And you and Jesus would spend time together, in this den?

JESUS is there with his guitar.

VERNON. I guess. Or just riding round, huntin' snakes, building planes out of cans…

JESUS sings a snatch of 'Your Cheatin' Heart' by Hank Williams; silly, happy.

Or bitchin'! At school they called him dumb but he was way smarter than any of them knew. An' funny, just a moron when it came to music!

He laughs. JESUS *line-dances.*

I tried to teach him some street, like, Lil Wayne, Snoop
Dogg, but he just went on wearing his shit, singing his heart
out, he didn't care!

VERNON *joins in* JESUS*'s song.* JESUS *falls away.*

He used not to care...

DR GOOSENS. Tell me what happened the day of the tragedy,
Vernon.

VERNON. I wasn't there!

DR GOOSENS. You're not on trial here, Vernon, please be
specific.

VERNON. I went to look for him.

DR GOOSENS. You followed Jesus? Why?

VERNON. He'd gotten used to a lot of shit at school for being
Mexican and – I think maybe he was gay or something –
anyway, he just ignored it but that day they put these pictures
of him on all the computers and... He ran, he ran from class.

DR GOOSENS. Did you find him?

VERNON. No, he'd gone, I was too late!

DR GOOSENS. What happened, Vernon?

VERNON. I needed the bathroom urgently!

DR GOOSENS. You were in the school bathroom?

VERNON. No.

DR GOOSENS. You took a leak outside school?

VERNON. Not a leak.

DR GOOSENS. You had a bowel movement, outside school, at
the time of the tragedy?

VERNON. I can be unpredictable.

DR GOOSENS. Have you told the court this?

VERNON. No.

DR GOOSENS. Forgive me, but doesn't a fresh stool identified as yours, situated away from the scene of the crime, rule you out as a suspect?

VERNON. Maybe. Anyway, my teacher knows I wasn't there.

DR GOOSENS. That's fine, then.

VERNON. Dr Goosens?

DR GOOSENS. Yes, Vernon?

VERNON. You won't tell the court about the stool, will you?

DR GOOSENS. What happens here, Vernon, is entirely confidential. How did you feel about Jesus being gay?

VERNON. Nothing. Never bothered me.

DR GOOSENS. Alrighty. So, you're unpredictable?

VERNON. It's no big deal…

DR GOOSENS. Is it a diagnosed condition such as – sphincter weakness?

VERNON. I don't know.

DR GOOSENS. Let's see what we can discover. Undress for me, please, come lie up here.

VERNON. Un-dress?

DR GOOSENS. Sure, to finish the examination. We psychiatrists are medical doctors first, you know.

DR GOOSENS *puts on latex gloves,* VERNON *takes his trousers off. Indicating his underpants.*

Off, please. On your stomach, spread your legs.

VERNON *goes behind the screen.*

Just relax, this procedure won't hurt a bit. You may even experience arousal...

DR GOOSENS *puts on 'Mars, the Bringer of War' from Holst's* The Planets, *then joins* VERNON *behind the screen. The music crescendos.*

VERNON. NO! (*Running away.*) Dr Goosens, non-negotiable schedule every day? Hell on fucken earth, I don't think so! (*Putting his clothes back on.*) That was not an okay doctor. Bail or no bail, I am nobody's animal fucken sex doll!

He's home.

LALLY. Uh, uh, uh, uh....

MOM. Uuuurgh, God, Lalito, unghh, ugn, ugh...

LALLY. Take me home, baby, uh, uh, uh...

MOM. Lally, Lally...

VERNON. Mom?

MOM (*flinging on her robe*). Oh, baby, hi! How was Dr Goofy?

LALLY (*still half-naked*). Psychiatrist cure you yet, Vern?

MOM. I just need to pay a visit to the little girls' room...

LALLY (*downing a bottle*). I can't tell you what you've put your mother through. Can you imagine if I'd not been around to pick up the pieces?

VERNON. Fuck off.

LALLY (*slaps him*). Fuckin' cuss at me.

VERNON. Shit, what are you, my dad?

LALLY. I'm sorry you didn't like the programme, because CNN did. They may even commission a whole series, in-depth coverage of the tragedy. We could turn your situation around three hundred and sixty degrees, Vern...

VERNON. Oh, a paradigm shift? Learn some fucken math.

Thumps off to his bedroom.

LALLY. Fancy a whole episode on finding the second gun. Any ideas, Vern, where that firearm might be?

VERNON (*from his room*). Fuck you!

(*To* JESUS, *who's singing again.*) Shut up, shit! Son of a stadium full of bitches, his toothbrush in my bathroom ain't cool! Why does she have such deadly fucking taste in men? Know what I'm gonna do? Know what? I'm gonna get the fuck shot of here. Hop a bus to Nana's and not even tell anyone. I swear she was dripping on the floor, eurgh!

His stomach cramps.

Oh, not again…

He gets to the toilet fast. Through the toilet door.

MOM. Vernon? Vernon?

VERNON. Yeah?

MOM. Are you alright?

VERNON. Sure I am.

MOM. Don't be sarcastic, Vernon. If you could just get a job, help me with the bills, be normal, everything would be fine again, I know it would.

VERNON. Playing happy families with Eulalio, after what he did?

MOM. What about what you did, bringing the Sheriff to the house?

VERNON. I didn't do anything!

MOM. This is special with Lally, Vernon, I know it.

VERNON. Mom, please…

MOM. Oh baby, you're jealous! I still love you best, you know…

PASTOR GIBBONS. Praise the Lord!

LALLY. Praise the Lord, Pastor!

PASTOR GIBBONS. Do I smell joy cakes for the Salvation
Sizzle?

LALLY. Sure do. Need a deputy for the day, Pastor?

> VERNON *emerges.*

> He'll give one hundred and fifty per cent.

> VERNON *is tied into a choir gown.*

VERNON. Huh?

> MOM *hands him the tray of joy cakes.*

> What the...?

MOM. Lally says it's important to show the community you're
making good.

VERNON. But I've done nothing wrong!

LALLY. Don't argue with your mother! Nice gown.

VERNON. Go fuck with your own kids.

EVERYBODY. Whoa!

> *'Will the Circle Be Unbroken' by Ada R Habershon,*
> *rearranged by A.P. Carter, kicks straight in.* VERNON *finds*
> *himself a very reluctant line-dancer in a whole line-up of*
> *dancers.* PASTOR GIBBONS *leads the first verse,* PAM *the*
> *second,* SHERIFF PORKORNEY *the third. Everyone joins*
> *in the choruses. There's a fancy dance-break where everyone*
> *shows off their skills.*

LALLY (*to camera, simultaneous with chorus*). And live from
the Salvation Sizzle, a fundraiser for victims of the Martirio
tragedy, we have Sheriff Porkorney. Tell us about the hunt,
Sheriff?

SHERIFF PORKORNEY. We got the dogs, we're lookin' for
drugs and a second firearm.

LALLY (*to camera*). So that's a hunt at Keeter's, the wasteland where Jesus Navarro used to spend his time. There's a barbecue after the hunt sponsored by Bar-B-Chew Barn, so bring the kids, should be a lot of fun.

VERNON. Keeter's? Shit...

KID IN BRACES (*singing to the tune of 'Will the Circle...'*). Twenty dollars...

VERNON. Joy cakes...

KID IN BRACES (*singing*). Twenty dollars...

VERNON. Joy cakes...

KID IN BRACES (*singing*). Get your T-shirts here today...

VERNON. Joy cakes...

KID IN BRACES (*singing*). To remind us – of the psycho – when he blew them kids away...

VERNON (*to* KID IN BRACES). Dude, wanna job for an hour?

KID IN BRACES. Not in a freakin' dress I don't.

VERNON. It ain't a dress, duh, just mind these cakes awhile.

KID IN BRACES. How much you payin'?

VERNON. You get commission on sales.

KID IN BRACES. Flat or indexed?

VERNON. Indexed to what? I'll give you eighteen per cent, flat.

KID IN BRACES. You for real, these stupid cakes?

VERNON. Dude!

KID IN BRACES. Twenty bucks, one hour.

VERNON. Yeah, like I'm Bill Gates or something...

KID IN BRACES. Twenty-five bucks or no deal. Thirty bucks, one calendar hour, final offer.

VERNON. Yah, shit.

He dumps his cakes on the KID IN BRACES *and is off on his bike. The final chorus of 'Where the Circle...' is sung by everyone.* MOM *finishes the song on her own at home, with a fragile couple of lines. The music shifts to jangly, Carteresque music.*

At Keeter's.

MR KEETER. Okay, son? Don't be touchin' nothin', could be dangerous.

VERNON. Sure, Mr Keeter, I was just cruising...

MR KEETER. I wouldn't recommend you cruise around here.

VERNON. Sir, I'm just –

MR KEETER. I don't recommend you bein' here just now, son.

VERNON. The thing is –

MR KEETER. The best thing I recommend is you don't be poking around here, this be a restricted area, go on now.

VERNON. Okay, Mr Keeter, sure, I'll get myself back into town, sir. (*Cycling off.*) So long, Mr Keeter!

Getting off his bike, creeping back. JESUS *creeps behind him.*

'*So long, Mr Keeter!*', pussyhole. (*To* JESUS.) Come on, man, come on, got to bury that gun or dig up my daddy.

He gets to the den, only to find he doesn't have the key.

Oh shit, the key!

ELLA. Shit, the key!

VERNON. Wha'?

ELLA. Hi, Bernie!

VERNON. Shhh, willya, I'm tryin to rest a little here, God!

ELLA. Looks like there's a door there, but you ain't got the key.

VERNON. Ella...

ELLA. That's what it looks like to me anyway...

VERNON. Ella, Ella, it's real urgent that nobody disturbs me right now, okay?

ELLA. Wanna see my South Pole?

VERNON. Shit, come on, willya? Hell!

ELLA. Can I just hang out, Bernie?

VERNON. Shhh! Anyway, my name's not even Bernie, duh.

ELLA. It is too Bernie, or something like that... it's Bernie or something like that.

VERNON. Listen, can we hang out some other time, can I owe you or something?

ELLA. If it's true and for actual real, maybe. Like when?

VERNON. Well, I don't know, just some time, next time, whatever.

ELLA. Promise?

VERNON. What?

ELLA. Promise me.

VERNON (*he means it*). Yeah, Ella, I promise.

ELLA. Hhmm.

VERNON. Fucken what?

ELLA. I love you, Bernie.

STEVEN. Spider, spider, spider!

VERNON. Shit!

ELLA. Shit!

VERNON. Shhh!

ELLA. Shhh!

VERNON. No, shhh!

ELLA. No, shhh! In here!

VERNON *and* ELLA *hide down a hole*.

TEAM LEADER. It's just nature, Steven, nothing to be afraid of.

STEVEN. Who cares about stoopid ol' nature?

TEAM LEADER. Not just nature, Steven, we're looking for a gun, which, as you know, can kill, so it's very important that we keep our eyes and ears open. Okay, team, stop here for the first item in your snack-packs! That's the item with the red label, the red-label item only.

Dogs bark.

TODD. I wanna toilet!

TEAM LEADER. I told you to go before we left the Barn, Todd. Just use one of those bushes.

TODD. I wanna real toilet!

TEAM LEADER. Well, you aren't gonna find one out here, this isn't the mall. Look, use that hole...

ELLA *stands up*.

ELLA. Hi.

TEAM LEADER. Ella Keeter! We've not seen you at school in a while.

ELLA. You can't use this hole, snakes sleep in it, you can't use it.

TEAM LEADER. Todd, wait, I think you better come with me...

ELLA. I said you can't use it!

MAY-MAY. It's the psycho-boy!

STEVEN. Does that boy kill children?

VERNON (*emerging from the hole*). Hi, Miss.

TEAM LEADER. Hi… I don't think I have your name – did Bar-B-Chew Barn assign you a team colour?

VERNON. Uh, green.

TEAM LEADER. Can't be green, it can only be a colour from the logo. I'll call Mrs Gurie, check the list. What's your name?

VERNON. Brad Pritchard.

TEAM LEADER. We already have a Brad Pritchard…

BRAD *emerges from the bushes*.

BRAD. Yeah, me. (*Taking a picture on his phone*.) Cool, the convict looking for his own gun!

TEAM LEADER (*on phone*). Vaine? I think we need some assistance…

BRAD (*imitating* ELLA). 'Hi, Bernie, wanna see my South Pole?'

ELLA. Hi, Brad, wanna see my snake?

She chases them. They all scream and run away.

Bernie?

VERNON. What?

ELLA. Bernie?

VERNON. What?

MR KEETER (*hollering*). Ella?

ELLA. See ya, Bernie.

VERNON. Weirdo.

JESUS *is back, shadowing* VERNON.

MR KEETER *and* ELLA *sing in the style of a Carter Family duet, 'He'll Keep His Word', an original song by Duncan Wisbey.*

VERNON (*to* JESUS). I hope they ain't home yet, Tom and Katie fucken Cruise.

He's home, it's quiet.

Hallelujah. Now, the key.

He heads to his room. The doorbell rings.

Fate pays attention to what you think, see, then paints a dick on your fucken forehead.

HEAVY (*offering his hand*). How are you? (*Grabbing* VERNON.) Where is he?

VERNON. Who?

HEAVY. Don't fuck with me, I know he stays here. The repairman!

VERNON. Which repairman?

HEAVY (*producing a business card*). Eulalio Ledesma Gutierrez! Bastard owes me money.

VERNON. Eulalio? (*Reading.*) 'TV Service Technician, Nacogdoches'?

HEAVY (*seeing* VERNON *is alone*). I'll be back.

VERNON (*to* JESUS). A TV repairman?
(*Going in to another rap.*)
O U Lally-O don't know what I know,
Got him cornered for sho in downtown Martirio,
So it's paradigmin' time in Nacogdoches,
Four beats in a line, fierce and ferocious,
Mistreatin' cheat, malign and atrocious,
Revenge is sweet, shoulda been mo' precautious,
Vern's gonna shine, boy, Vern's feelin fine,
You'll never fuck my mom again,
Expialidocious.

You got a fucken break, Vern! (*Punching the number into the phone, singing to the tune of 'Will the Circle…'*) Para-di-igm, para-di-igm, para-di-aa-igm…

The music for 'Crazy' by Patsy Cline starts, led by JESUS.

LALLY'S MOM (*on phone*). He-llo?

VERNON (*on phone*). Uh, hello, I'm wondering if Eulalio Ledesma works there?

LALLY'S MOM. Who is this? I only have what's left in my purse…

VERNON. Ma'am, I didn't mean to trouble you, I thought this was a business number?

LALLY'S MOM. I had cards printed for my boy, Lalo…

VERNON. Your son?

LALLY'S MOM. All I have is eight dollars for groceries and they're suing over the camera he hired…

VERNON. I'm real sorry I troubled you, ma'am.

LALLY'S MOM. He has to bring the camera back, I don't know where he's gone…

VERNON. Have you not seen him on TV?

LALLY'S MOM. Young man, I've been blind for thirty years!

VERNON. Oh, ma'am, I'm so sorry…

MOM *approaches, laughing.*

MOM. Oh-ho-ho, Lalito, stop!

VERNON. I have a number here you can call him on, do you have a pen, or, uh, whatever you use to write things down? It's 7356398622 – okay, ma'am?

LALLY'S MOM. Yes…

VERNON. Okay?

MOM *and* LALLY *are in.*

LALLY. Babe, have you seen my therapy bag?

MOM. No, babe, I think you're all out of your gin-sling things. Hi, guys!

LEONA (*arriving*). Hi, Doris! Hi, Lally... (*Re:* BRAD*'s pretend gun.*) Put that down, Bradley.

MOM. Babe, I found one!

LALLY. Thanks, Vanessa, you're indispensable.

LEONA. Vanessa?

MOM. Well, we can't say much yet, can we, Lalito?

LALLY. Just that the network was impressed with her television debut. We could be seeing a lot more of her once the right strategies are in place. (*Crooning into her ear.*) Vanessa Le Bourget...

LEONA. Wow, isn't that weird because, did I tell you guys, my new dialogue coach is sending my reel to the networks, right after I get back from Hawaii? Wow.

LALLY (*to* MOM). I can't wait to share you with the crew in New York, they're gonna love you, those guys.

VERNON (*emerging from behind the sofa*). Do you think they'll like her in Nacogdoches?

LALLY. Whoa!

MOM *and* LEONA. Vernon!

PASTOR GIBBONS (*entering*). Praise the Lord!

LALLY. C'mon on in, Preacher.

PASTOR GIBBONS. Am I disrupting anything?

LALLY. Your timing's perfect, Pastor. Vernon, perhaps you'll explain to the Pastor why you abandoned his charity stall today?

VERNON. Stomach ache.

LALLY. Surely, a person bailed for murder would do better to...

VERNON. I'm not on bail for murder, fuck!

LALLY. Control yourself!

MOM *starts bawling*.

LEONA. Such aggression, just like his big Meskin psychopath
buddy…

VERNON. Guess what? (*Furious, producing* LALLY'*s business
card*.) Everybody, I called Eulalio's office today and guess
who answered? His blind momma! Did you know he's
actually a TV repairman who works out of his momma's
home in Nacogdoches?

LALLY. Oh, please.

VERNON. She's gonna call here, and when she does, ask her
where he got his camera from, ask her about his debts –

LALLY (*sweating*). The evil lies coming from this child's
mouth! Hands up who ever heard of a features reporter
moonlighting as a repairman? No? And why might that be?

BRAD. You wouldn't need to, with all your money from
reportin'.

MOM. That's right, Brad!

VERNON. Who said he moonlighted? He's not a reporter, he's
just a repairman, look at the card!

LALLY *pursues* VERNON *and the card*.

LALLY. Ladies, this is preposterous, have you ever seen me
repair a TV?

MOM. No.

LALLY. Have you seen me on TV, presenting a features report?

LEONA. We were in it with you!

LALLY. Thank you. Now, in light of everything we've just heard
and, frankly, for our own protection, I'm calling the police.

MOM. Oh no, Lally, / please.

VERNON. Wait, she's gonna call / right now...

LALLY. I'm sorry, Vanessa, it's my duty.

The phone rings.

I'll get that.

VERNON *gets there first.*

VERNON. Mom, come take this call!

MOM. Hello? Mr Ledesma, sure, may I say who's calling? Renée?

LALLY. Renée?

VERNON (*grabbing the phone*). Mrs Ledesma?

MOM. Vernon!

LALLY (*seizing the phone*). Hello, Renée? Hi! Yeah, things are a little crazy down here... I got the series? Oh, fantastic! (*A moment of animal celebration.*) Yes! Conditional on what? Not a challenge, we have the firearm piece, the living suspect, the townsfolk coming to terms with their grief – it can spin-off in a thousand directions.

MOM. I still can't decide between Vanessa or Peaches...

LALLY. Sure, sure, thank you, *à bientôt*, Renée! (*Dropping the receiver back.*) Woo-hoo! Just before we open the champagne, pretty outlandish behaviour we saw there, Vernon – damn scary, actually, in light of everything.

VERNON. Fuck you to hell.

MOM. Vernon Gregory, what is wrong with you?

LALLY. Simple compassion dictates it's time to turn this boy over to someone who can help.

VERNON. You're the one who needs help, motherfucker!

LALLY. But you're the one under a psychiatric order. How you
concocted that Nacogdoches story! The crew back in the
Apple will just love that! I might have to call them, right
after I contact the Sheriff.

MOM. No, Lally, please… I mean, he had stomach ache, he has
this condition –

The phone rings, LALLY *answers in a flash.*

LALLY. Le Bourget residence?

VERNON. Press the speaker button, Mom.

MOM. Vernon, cope, for God's sake!

LALLY. I'm sorry…

VERNON. Hit the button!

LALLY. You must have the wrong number.

He dives round LALLY*, presses the speaker button, protects
it.* LALLY'S MOM*'s voice sails out the speakers.*

LALLY'S MOM (*on phone*). Lalo? Oh my God, Lalo, I ran out
of groceries…

LALLY. Oh, oh, it's you…

LALLY'S MOM. *Es que no queda nada, Eulalio, hasta mi
cama se lo han llevado…* [It's just that there's nothing left,
Eulalio, they've even taken my bed…]

VERNON (*to* LALLY'S MOM). Tell him in English!

LALLY *kicks* VERNON, *switches the speaker off.*

LALLY. Oh, you poor souls, I left strict instructions with the
network to keep up my charity visits while I was away…

VERNON *tries to switch it on again,* LALLY *keeps him at
bay.* BRAD *joins in the game on* LALLY's *side.*

I know, sweetheart, but mental illness can be cured, that's
why I contribute, why I share myself with your cause, you
and all the other beautiful ladies at the home… Goodbye,
I'm thinking of you!

LALLY *slams down the phone. It rings again. He rips it out the socket.*

I guess I have something to confess.

'Crazy' finally kicks in.

Some time ago I decided to share my resources with the less fortunate.

PASTOR GIBBONS. Amen.

LALLY. I'd been so ambitious, so wrapped up in me, then I became involved with real people, real problems. The voice you heard is one of my ladies, one of my Sunshine Souls.

LEONA. God.

LALLY. Tragic, isn't it? Confined through no fault of her own. They all are.

VERNON. Bullshit.

MOM. Vernon, that's enough!

LEONA. Were you supporting them?

LALLY. Maybe things'd be better if I wasn't, there are just so many wretched lives to care for and I have so little to give…

PASTOR GIBBONS. No, son, you're giving the greatest gift of all, Christian love.

LALLY. Thanks very much, Pastor. So if you see me a little short of cash, now you know why. I feel so guilty having anything at all. But I guess the real tragedy is, now they know where I'm staying.

MOM. Well, why is that tragic…?

LALLY. The home's strictest rule is non-disclosure of carers' identities. If they know where I am, I could be prevented from giving in the future.

VERNON. Oh no, you fucker…

LALLY. It means I'll have to move along.

MOM. Well, God, Lally, no, I mean, no, God…

'Crazy' lifts off and takes flight, threading the lines of song between the lines of dialogue.

LEONA, PASTOR GIBBONS and BRAD form the backing group to JESUS's song.

LALLY. I'm sorry, Doris, but this is bigger than the two of us.

MOM. But we can disconnect the phone, change the number, Lalito? You can't walk out after this month of bliss.

LALLY. Week of bliss, *week*. Maybe if Vernon hadn't called the home, if he didn't harbour such a grudge against me, but things'll only get more challenging after I call the Sheriff.

MOM starts to sob.

LEONA. There's space at my place.

LALLY. My God, the pure charity of this town…

MOM. Well, but, but, the home might find you there as well, that woman, she could just as easy find you at Leona's as here…

LEONA. I'm unlisted, I have call-screening and closed-circuit security.

MOM. Well, but, Vernon could just as easily give Leona's number to the patients, couldn't you, Vernon, just give her number to the home?

VERNON. Ma, the guy's a goddamn psycho!

MOM. See? See his behaviour?

Another line of 'Crazy' escalates MOM's gathering hysteria.

He could call them right now! I think Lally and I should take a room at the Seldome for a while, Lalito? Do all those other things you wanted to do…

LALLY. Seldome's full.

MOM. I was married at the Seldome, they'd always find space for me…

LEONA (*jangling keys*). Offer's open.

MOM. Where's the Seldome's number?

LALLY. Doris, that's not all. (*Pulling out* VERNON*'s joint.*) Vernon didn't do such a good job of hiding this. Illegal drugs. You'll understand now why I can't be associated with the boy.

BRAD. Enjoy jail!

LALLY (*privately to* VERNON). Relish your reefer, Vernon Paradigm Little. I already filmed the drugs episode. So long, Doris.

The singing continues, no longer interspersed with the dialogue but now concurrent with the scene of LALLY *leaving, as below.* JESUS *sings, with full backing from everyone.*

MOM. Lally, no, please, don't go…

LALLY. Let go, come on now, let me go…

MOM. No, Lall-eee…

LALLY. Don't make a scene now, Doris…

They continue to-ing and fro-ing, improvising, MOM *begging, offering sexual favours, alongside the song, until* LALLY *gives* MOM *a final kiss and grope before detaching.*

I'll be back for my stuff!

The song stops. There's silence.

VERNON (*to us*). Let me introduce myself, Vernon Genius Little. My best friend put a gun in his mouth and blew off his head, my classmates are dead and I'm being blamed for it and now…

MOM *breathes in…*

I just broke my mama's heart.

…then lets out a long wail. The song picks up again, concurrent with the dialogue.

MOM. Lord God in heaven, I am serene, I am positive, I will
have a new refrigerator, I will have it, I will have it, please
let me have it, God in Heaven, bring Lally back, bring him
back, please, please, please bring him back...

VERNON. Mom?

MOM. Well, shut up, Vernon! You did this to me, all this
fucking shit! (*To the* SINGERS.) Shut up, fuckin' fuck off!

They stop, slink off sheepishly.

VERNON. I'm sorry, Ma.

She cries voicelessly.

Mom, please? You sound like a cat.

MOM. Papa always told me I'd amount to nothing. And your
daddy said the same, again and again...

VERNON. Don't, Mom...

MOM. Well, look at me, it's true, it's always been true. Do I
look like I deserve a place on this earth?

VERNON. Come on...

MOM. I'm stupid, I'm ugly, I'm useless and I always have been!

VERNON. You're not useless...

MOM. I can't even pay the electric bill, how useless is that?
Crap! Vernon, you're all I have in the world. If you could've
seen your daddy's face when he knew you were a boy... there
wasn't a taller man in the whole of Texas. We used to talk
about all the great things you were going to be when you grew
up... Ah well. I guess Lally will be calling the Sheriff now.

VERNON. Well, at least I'm innocent.

MOM. Oh Vern, I mean, huh.

VERNON. What do you mean, 'huh'? I didn't do anything,
Mom.

MOM. Well, but surely the damage is done? You had that awful catalogue and now these illegal drugs...

VERNON. That was your goddam catalogue!

MOM. I know it was mine, what got into you? Was it something that Jesus Navarro boy put you up to?

VERNON. I think I'll take some air.

MOM. What do you call this?

VERNON. I mean at the park or something.

MOM. Vernon, it's nearly eleven o'clock.

VERNON. Ma, for chrissakes...

MOM. Don't you cuss your mother, Vernon!

VERNON. I ain't cussing!

MOM. Honestly, Vernon Gregory, if your daddy was here right now...

VERNON. What, we'd be covered in bruises?

MOM *backs down.*

I'm going.

MOM *really wails now.*

What did I do, I'm only going to the park?

MOM. There must be a thousand kids / in this town –

VERNON. Not so goddamn / many now –

MOM. But you don't see them at the park in the middle of the night, because they're from normal families and in vacation they get up in the morning and earn money. Most of the boys I know have jobs already!

VERNON. Like which boys, Ma?

MOM. Like – Randy and Eric!

VERNON. Randy and Eric are dead! I'm going to the park.

He goes, MOM *cries. He goes again, she cries louder. Finally he turns back.*

Mom? Mom? Okay, I got a job.

MOM. Oh, you did?

VERNON. I wasn't even going to tell you, but… I already talked to Mr Keeter about it, so, hey.

MOM. Mr Keeter? Well, when do you start?

VERNON. Tomorrow.

MOM. Doing what?

VERNON. Just – helping out.

MOM. Really? Oh, but don't you have to see Dr Goosens every day?

VERNON. Uh…

MOM. If the Sheriff comes for you again, Vern…

VERNON. I already fixed it, I can start late, after Dr Goosens.

MOM. How quickly will you get paid, Vern? The power's going to be disconnected…

VERNON. Uh, I can probably get an advance.

MOM. With no work history?

VERNON. Sure, so now can I go to the park?

MOM. I never said you couldn't.

PAM (*arriving in her Mercury*). Y'all die and nobody told me? I been calling your darn number since Adam and Eve.

VERNON. Phone's broke.

MOM (*crying again*). Lalito's gone!

PAM. Took his time. You hungry? This food's getting soggy. C'mon, Doris, or I'll call Lolly, tell him about your herpes.

MOM. Shit, Palmyra, God.

> PAM *roars with laughter.*

> You're just too damn perky. It's important to hurt sometimes.

PAM. Want me to push ya down the stairs? Haugh, haugh, haugh.

MOM. Did you say you brought food?

> VERNON *flies back to* MR KEETER*'s on his bike,* JESUS *following, with twangly 'He'll Keep His Word' accompaniment.*

VERNON (*to* JESUS). Smart. I invent an imaginary job with an imaginary start time and imaginary pay! I need cash fast.

> *He's there.*

> Si? Silas?

SILAS. Shill my wincer, son, what time d'you call this?

VERNON. Sorry, Si, but I got some real big business to run by you.

SILAS. You have? Let's see what you got there...

VERNON. Here's the thing, Si – no hard stuff, on account o' the police took –

SILAS (*closing his door*). So what the...?

VERNON. Wait, Si, Si, I'm busting the business! I'm gonna tell you where you can get all the amputee porn you want –

SILAS. Hell, son –

VERNON. No, wait, Si, see these internet addresses?

SILAS. Internet?

VERNON. I wrote everything down, all the instructions –

SILAS. Nah.

> *Slam goes his door.*

VERNON. 'Limbless Love'…

It opens again.

'Tasty Torsos'…

SILAS. Mm. How much ya wantin'?

VERNON. A hundred bucks.

SILAS. A six-pack.

VERNON. A six-pack? Si, the other kids'll wanna kill me after I bust the business like this… fifty!

SILAS. Six-packa Coors, I'll go git it.

VERNON. Twenty?

SILAS hands him the beer, disappears.

Gee thanks, I'll give these to my mom, she can send them to the electric company. What is wrong with this fucking life? You do nothing but trouble sticks to you like tongue on dry pussy.

A dog barks.

(*Barking back angrily.*) Wrugh, wrugh, wrugh! Who do you think you are, god of the fucking barking club? (*To* JESUS.) A six-pack o' beer, a reefer and no cash. As you used to say – when you're down on your ass, get wasted fast.

ELLA. Hi, Bernie.

VERNON. Shit.

ELLA. Whatcha doin'?

VERNON. Hanging out.

ELLA. Whatcha doin' really?

VERNON. Hanging out, I toldja… You shouldn't even be here.

ELLA. You're getting loaded and wasted off your ass. Anyway, you promised. Fuck, Bernie, you're just like an alcoholic.

VERNON. I'm not 'just like an alcoholic' and my name's not Bernie.

ELLA. What is it then? It's something like Bernie…

VERNON. No, my name's nothing like Bernie, not in the minimum.

ELLA. I'll go ask my dad what the name of the guy is who's over here smoking weed and drinking beer.

VERNON. Name's John, okay?

ELLA. John? No it ain't. It ain't John, not John at all. You're not called John, you ain't…

VERNON. Ella, Ella… I don't want to make a big deal out of anything today, okay? I'm just here, trying to chill on my own, okay?

ELLA. Not with a name like John you ain't. You ain't John, no way…

VERNON. Well, whatever, okay?

ELLA. See? I knew it was Bernie. Can I have a beer?

VERNON. No.

ELLA. How come?

VERNON. Because you're only eight.

ELLA. I ain't too so eight, I'm nearly fuckin' fifteen.

VERNON. Still too young to drink alcoholic beverages.

ELLA. Well, you're too young to drink and smoke weed, fuck.

VERNON. No I ain't.

ELLA. Yes you are, how old are you?

VERNON. Twenty-two.

ELLA. You are not, you are not fuckin' twenty-two. Fuck, it's hot out here.

She lifts her skirt too high.

VERNON. Ella, c'mon, will ya?

He starts to leave.

ELLA. I'll go to the shop and scream. I'll tell Daddy what you did to me after all that weed and beer, Bernie.

VERNON. Oh shit, okay, Ella, here, have some beer.

They share. A harmonious riff from 'He'll Keep His Word' wafts in. She inches closer. He feels her warmth. She gets too close. He backs off.

You need a bath, El.

ELLA. How come you don't fool around, Bernie, you a pillow-biter or what?

VERNON. No, I just think you're too young, that's all.

ELLA. Guys a whole lot older than you want to fool around with me.

VERNON. Yeah, right, like who?

ELLA. Like...

VERNON. Exactly, I don't fucken think so!

ELLA. Yeah they do, a whole shitloada guys!

VERNON. C'mon, Ella...

ELLA. Mr Deutschman would, I know that, I know that too damn well.

VERNON. Fuck, El, Mr Deutschman's around eight hundred years old.

ELLA. So? He's older'n you and he'd even pay for it.

VERNON. Yeah, right. Pay for it?

The beginning chords of 'Sailing' by Christopher Cross start. ELLA runs off to get a camera. JESUS is there lurking but VERNON doesn't see him.

ELLA. Guess what? (*Lifting her dress*.) They're clean!

VERNON. Nice work, El. Ella, it's just look and touch, ol
Nothing heavy. Call me if he goes too far.

ELLA. Chill out, Bernie, I'm the one with the poles, remember?
Go on. Mr Deutschman?

MR DEUTSCHMAN*'s listening to a little radio.*

MR DEUTSCHMAN. My, what's this here, a visitor? Come in,
come on in, it's Ella, isn't it?

ELLA. I got something for you, Mr Deutschman. Look! New
panties. You wanna see my South Pole or my North Pole?
Wow, your hands are cold… Ha, that tickles!

She grins. VERNON*'s camera flashes.*

VERNON. It's okay, Mr Deutschman, I'm real sorry to barge in
like this. We're not here to make trouble. The young lady is
here by choice and I'm just here with her. A little cash is all
we require, three hundred dollars, for instance, then I'll leave
the two of you to hang out some more, and, sir? You can
have this photograph and we'll never come by again or say a
word to anyone, that's our solemn promise to you.

We see LALLY *through the window.*

ELLA. Sure is!

MR DEUTSCHMAN (*handing over his wallet*). Take it.

VERNON. Is this all you have, sir? (*He peels off ten dollars,
puts it back.*) We don't want to clean you out or anything.
Okay, so I'll leave you two alone…

LALLY. Well, hi!

ELLA. Bernie!

MR DEUTSCHMAN. No…!

VERNON *and* ELLA *run.* LALLY *intercepts them.*

LALLY. My, but you're such a career man these days.

VERNON *launches himself at* LALLY.

Ooohf! Sack of shit!

ELLA *pinches his camera, runs off.*

My camera! Give it back, fucken' pedo-bait!

VERNON (*handing* MR DEUTSCHMAN *the photograph*).
Destroy it, sir, and whatever you do, don't trust that guy!

ELLA *runs in, hands* LALLY*'s camera to* MR
DEUTSCHMAN, VERNON *grabs her and runs.*

LALLY. Wanna play in the real world, cocksucker? (*On phone.*)
Sheriff? It's Lalito.

VERNON. El – (*He kneels next to her.*) El… I have seven
fucken seconds to plan the rest of my life, I have to trust you
with something.

ELLA. You can trust me, Bernie.

VERNON. We got a hundred and eighty dollars, that's ninety
apiece. That's yours, that's mine.

*He picks out ten dollars, puts it in his pocket, hands the rest
to* ELLA.

Can you take eighty of mine to 17 Beulah Drive? You'll have
to tie up your hair, change your clothes, sneak down there
like a shadow – can you do that for me?

ELLA. Sure I can, what're you gonna do?

VERNON. He's on my back, I have to go.

ELLA. I'll come with you.

VERNON. The hell you will, and Ella…

ELLA. Yeah?

VERNON. If you see my ole lady, tell her I'm sorry to leave,
an' – no, Ella, don't say anything, just slide the cash under
the door, okay?

She counts out her ninety dollars and stuffs them into his hands.

ELLA. Here.

VERNON. That's yours.

ELLA. I don't need it.

VERNON. But, Ella...

She plants a kiss on his lips.

ELLA. I love you, Bernie.

She runs off. There's a flash of blue light. SHERIFF PORKORNEY *appears,* VERNON *hides.*

SHERIFF PORKORNEY (*calling*). Eulalio? Lalito?

LALLY. Over here, Sheriff, the boy's here.

SHERIFF PORKORNEY *walks forwards,* LALLY *shoots him three times, dead.*

That'll show you, Vernon Little, suck on that piece of market positioning, fucken big man.

Help! Vernon Little shot the Sheriff, help!

VERNON (*horribly shocked*). Shit. Shit.

'Sailing' intro picks up momentum. VERNON *runs on to the motorway, narrowly escaping being run over. A bus rumbles. His voice is up an octave.*

Stop!

'Pschhsss.'

BUS DRIVER. You in trouble?

VERNON. Where's this bus goin'?

BUS DRIVER. Houston.

VERNON. Houston's good, my friend lives in Houston.

BUS DRIVER. Hold on, you can't just hail the service any old place…

VERNON. You already stopped!

BUS DRIVER. I could get in trouble for that –

VERNON. Please, you don't understand…

BUS DRIVER. Well, if you get on between stops I'd have to charge you the whole fare from, like…

VERNON. Sure, sure, whatever.

He slaps down half his cash, climbs on. Chooses a seat, finds JESUS *there, changes seat.*

No, partner, please, please give me some peace…

To JESUS, *who has followed him.*

Why, man? Why did you do it?

LITTLE OLD LADY. You alright?

VERNON. Sure, I'll be okay…

As she takes her hand away, VERNON *cranes for more.*

LITTLE OLD LADY. I'm so sorry you have troubles. I'm right over here if you need company, right over here.

The LITTLE OLD LADY *and* JESUS *sing 'Sailing' as a duet, with a capella support from other* PASSENGERS. *The song surrounds* VERNON *and his grief.*

End of Act One.

ACT TWO

*Big orchestrated news music fires out from an upgraded
television.* LALLY*'s arm is in a sling.*

LALLY (*on TV*). New shock for the Texas community of
Martirio. The town's Sheriff, Sheriff Porkorney, has been
shot dead. A full police search is on for runaway, Vernon
Gregory Little, the sole suspect for this horrific crime. Mr
Little is also suspected of being the accomplice to Jesus
Navarro's murders at the town's high school.

Phone rings. CHRISSIE, TAYLOR*'s flatmate, picks up.
Loud dance music plays in background.*

CHRISSIE. Hello?

VERNON. Taylor? Hi, it's Vern.

CHRISSIE. Taylor, it's Burn.

TAYLOR. Burn?

CHRISSIE. Worm?

TAYLOR. Sperm?

CHRISSIE (*cracking up*). Sperm!

TAYLOR (*answering*). Tayla.

VERNON. Uh, hi, it's Vern.

TAYLOR. Vern?

VERNON. Vern Little, remember me?

TAYLOR. Vern Little? Like, gee…

CHRISSIE *is in quiet hysterics.*

VERNON. Vernon Gregory Little, from Martirio? You might've seen me on the news…

TAYLOR. Oh, Martirio? I'm real sorry, I heard about the massacre and all, but I usually only watch, like, cable, you know?

CHRISSIE. Anal Intruder Channel!

TAYLOR. Fuck off, Chrissie, God.

VERNON. Uh, well, I'm the messy-haired dude from outside the senior party that time, I kept some stuff of yours for you…

TAYLOR. Oh hey, Vern! You took care of me that night, like, boy, did I overdo it or what!

VERNON. Hell, no big deal…

TAYLOR (*to* CHRISSIE). Chrissie, will you get the fuck out of here and close the door! Sorry, what were you saying?

VERNON. Thing is, I'm in Houston, and I thought maybe we could grab a coffee or something?

TAYLOR. Gee, Vern, I'm like, wow, you know? Maybe next time.

VERNON. Uh, what about lunchtime or something?

TAYLOR. Look, it's sweet of you to call…

VERNON. Taylor, listen – I've jumped bail, I'm on the run.

TAYLOR. Holy shit, like –

She turns the music down.

What happened?

VERNON. I can't really talk on the phone.

TAYLOR. God, but you seemed like, wow, you know, such a quiet guy.

VERNON. Maybe not so quiet, as it turns out, not so damn quiet any more.

TAYLOR. But you're only, like, fourteen, no?

VERNON. Uh, seventeen actually, these days, so yeah. I guess I must've just snapped against the injustice and all.

TAYLOR. Oh my God... You want to talk?

VERNON. Uh...

TAYLOR. I'll understand if you don't. Like, are you guilty?

VERNON. Nah, but try telling them that.

TAYLOR. Is it robbery or something?

VERNON. Murder.

TAYLOR. Eek. You okay?

VERNON. Tay, this might seem sudden, but I have something assertive to ask you...

TAYLOR. Assertive?

VERNON. Uh, it's just that I'm, like, going to Mexico an' – I wondered if you'd like to come –

CHRISSIE *turns the music up.*

TAYLOR. Chrissie, I mean it, get the fuck out of here! Sorry, what were you sayin'?

VERNON (*losing his nerve*). Heck, Tay, I'm being real selfish here, I didn't even find out how you're doing?

TAYLOR. You're killing me, like, God. I'm just here, trying out for stuff. I'm lookin' to work on TV but didn't get casted yet... just like, whatever, you know? And I'm seeing this doctor, can you believe? He's an older guy, obviously, but I'm sooo in love.

VERNON. Hey, wow.

TAYLOR.Yeah, he drives like an original Stingray, whatever, and in November we're doing Colorado for my birthday...

News music.

VERNON. Taylor, hold on...

LALLY (*on TV*). Attention now turns to the whereabouts of Vernon Gregory Little, the youngest serial killer ever known in the state of Texas.

VERNON. Tay, I have to go.

LALLY (*on TV*). After gunning down Sheriff Porkorney, it seems Little embarked on a killing spree, leaving families devastated across the state.

TAYLOR. What were you going to assertively ask me?

LALLY (*on TV*). Authorities warn that the suspect may be armed and is highly dangerous. The task of securing the state's borders will continue long into the night.

TAYLOR.Vern? Call me.

BORDER GUARD. Passport please.

VERNON (*wired, urgent*). Passport?

BORDER GUARD. Yes, passport please.

VERNON. But – I'm American.

BORDER GUARD. Driver licence?

VERNON. Well, no, I'm an American, visiting your beautiful country and all...

BORDER GUARD. You have identification? You can't enter Mexico without identification.

VERNON. But I have to meet my parents, see? They came down early and I had to stay back and now they're over there waiting, like, they're probably worried and all.

BORDER GUARD. You parents on vacation?

VERNON. Yeah, vacation.

BORDER GUARD. Where you parents?

VERNON. Tijuana…

BORDER GUARD. Ti-juana?

VERNON. Uh-huh.

BORDER GUARD. Is the other side of Mexico.

VERNON. No, that's right, but they came the other way, see, and I was here so I have to go across and meet them there, you know?

BORDER GUARD. Where in Tijuana?

VERNON. The hotel.

BORDER GUARD. Which hotel?

VERNON. The… heck, I have it written down…

BORDER GUARD. Call you parents, they come for you.

VERNON. I don't have a phone and anyway I thought our two countries were in a pact or something, I thought Americans could just walk right over…

BORDER GUARD. How I know you American?

A patrol car flashes.

VERNON. Ma'am, señora, I'm American, look at me, you can check my wallet and everything…

BORDER GUARD. Wallet? (*She empties it.*) This all the money you have?

VERNON. Yeah.

She pockets it, hands the wallet back.

BORDER GUARD. Welcome to Mexico.

There is complete silence. Mexico opens up around VERNON, boundless and dark. JESUS is there. He's changed his shirt.

VERNON. Never imagined I'd get here without you, Jesus.

Out of the darkness, a bar emerges.

PELAYO. *¿Y que? ¿No hay mujeres?* [And – are there no women?]

BARTENDER. *El unico mujeres eres tu, cabrón. Agáchate...* [The only woman here is you, man. Bend over...]

PELAYO. Hee, hee, heh, heh, heh, heh.

BARTENDER (*seeing* VERNON). *¿Qué quieres?* [What d'you want?]

VERNON. Uh – no money.

PELAYO. Heh, heh, heh, heh... (*He spits.*)

BARTENDER. Huh, huh, huh, huh. (*He spits.*)

PELAYO *puts his hand in his pocket and pulls out some Mexican notes.*

PELAYO. *Esto para tus pantalones.* [For your trousers.]

BARTENDER. 'Yes'! Hurh, hurh, hurh.

PELAYO. Heh, heh, heh...

BARTENDER *sets about removing* VERNON's *trousers while* PELAYO *unbuttons his own.*

VERNON. Oh, fuck, not this again....

VERNON *is dragged behind the bar.* BARTENDER *plays guitar. Finally, they emerge.*

PELAYO. Ta-da!

PELAYO *is kitted out in* VERNON's *clothes,* VERNON *in* PELAYO's. PELAYO *howls with laughter.*

'Nice!' *Por fin pareces Gringo!* [Now you look American.] Yah, hah, hah, hah!

They improvise, 'You looking at me?', etc., in Mexican-Spanish.

BARTENDER. *¿Quieres beber algo?* [What do you want?]

VERNON. Uh… (*Hugely relieved.*) Tequila? *Tres, tres tequilas!*

BARTENDER *smiles, pours three shots.*

BARTENDER. *Salud!*

PELAYO. *Salud!*

VERNON. *Salud!*

They spit, they drink.

PELAYO, BARTENDER *and* VERNON *speed through Mexico in* PELAYO*'s truck, singing heartily 'Ring of Fire' by June Carter and Merle Kilgore, but with Mexican-Spanish lyrics.* JESUS *sits in the back, joining in. Mexico unravels and explodes around them.*

TAYLOR (*on phone*). Tayla?

VERNON. Tay, hi, it's Vern.

TAYLOR. Oh my God.

VERNON. Tay, listen…

TAYLOR. Like, I can't believe I'm talking to a serial killer.

VERNON. I ain't no killer…

TAYLOR. Yeah, right, they have bodies mounted up all the way to Victoria! Where are you?

VERNON. Uh – Mexico…

TAYLOR. Have you seen back home? It's like some major festival, the town is buzzing, they've opened a juice bar, a sushi bar…

VERNON. Tay, I'm on a public phone…

TAYLOR. You need cash, right? I have, like, six hundred put away for my vacation.

VERNON. Are you serious? It'd save my fucken life…

TAYLOR. You talking dirty to me, killer? But, hey, where to wire it, did you stop somewhere? And what if they, like, you know…

VERNON. Shit, I guess that's right.

TAYLOR. Vern, call me from, like, a city or a big hotel, I'll check with Western Union.

Now they're driving through rural Mexico. Hills, long roads, dry plains, cacti. They sing the final verse of their Spanish 'Ring of Fire'.

MOM (*on telephone*). Hello?

VERNON. Mom, it's Vern…

MOM. Oh my God, Vernon, where are you?

VERNON. I'm sorry, Mom, I can't tell you.

MOM. All this death, Vernon, the Sheriff and all those other people…

VERNON. I didn't kill anybody, I saw Lally shoot the sheriff!

MOM. Oh, don't be childish, Vernon, just come home!

Back in the truck. The landscape is more urban as they approach Acapulco. The traffic is chaos. There's a Mexican motorway ballet, very different in character to the Martirio Highway. Everybody sings 'Guadalajara', the famous mariachi song.

TAYLOR (*on phone*). Tayla.

VERNON. Mexico calling.

TAYLOR. Hi, killer.

VERNON. You okay?

TAYLOR (*sniffly*). I'm just, like, what the fuck, you know? This damn guy I was dating…

VERNON. The doctor?

TAYLOR. Yeah, the so-called doctor. Anyway, where are you?

VERNON. Acapulco.

TAYLOR. Lemme see the map. Are you, like, by the beach?

VERNON. Yeah, the main boulevard.

TAYLOR. Okay, there's a Western Union agent at a big hotel called the Miguel Acapulco.

VERNON. I'll make it up to you, Tay.

TAYLOR. But listen, it's Sunday tomorrow, I can't get the cash till Monday, and babe –

'Beep', the phone cuts off. The truck makes its final descent to Guerrero, VERNON *asleep on* PELAYO's *shoulder. The truck splutters to a halt, greeted by* PELAYO'S WIFE, *chickens, pigs, dogs and the ocean.*

PELAYO. *Hola, amor de mi vida.* [Hello, love of my life.] (*To the animals.*) *Vete, saquense de aqui.* [Move it, move it, go on, get going.]

PELAYO'S WIFE (*freaking out completely at the chickens*). *Ándale, gallinas vergas de mierda, hijas de sus putisimas pulgosas madres, saquense a la chingada!* [Go on, shit-cunting chickens, daughters of your most whorish and flea-ridden mothers, fuck away off!]

Then a lingering kiss for PELAYO.

Hola, mi amor... [Hello, my love]

VERNON. Wow.

PELAYO. *Una cerveza para nuestro amiguito, Brad Pritchard.* [A beer for our young friend here, Brad Pritchard.]

She offers her hand and a beer to VERNON.

PELAYO'S WIFE. Hola, Brad!

The moon is high, the waves are lapping. PELAYO *and his* WIFE *sing a soulful Mexican duet, while dancing together.*

sits near VERNON, *humming a backing to their*

VERNON (*to* JESUS). Mexico, man. It's like someone flicked the switch on the fucken jacuzzi! Turns out back home is a lukewarm tub with no bubbles. You know, when all this shit is over an' everyone stops being so fucken wrong about everything, I'm gonna get Taylor and my mom out here. This, right here, is real life. No one laughs at your fucken haircut or your shoes or who your best friend is, down in Guerrero. Know what I'm gonna do, know what? I'm gonna find me a Mexican beach hut, an' Taylor, in nothing but panties – not burlesque or anything, just simple cotton ones – can hang in the salt breeze while I catch us some fish to cook on the fire.

He catches PELAYO*'s eye.*

You don't know what I'm babbling about but I love you, Pelayo, Pelayo's wife, who's name I'm too spazzo American to fucken remember – I love you all!

PELAYO. *No entiendo ni una palabra pero ¡lo quiero, lo quiero como hermano!* [I don't know what he's talking about, but I love him! I love him like a brother!]

VERNON. I'm in paradise, an' – guess what? It's my birthday!

PELAYO. *Buenas noches, que sueñes con los angelitos.* [Goodnight, sweet dreams.]

PELAYO'S WIFE (*seductively calling him to bed*). Pelayo…

PELAYO. *Muy, buenas noches…!* [Goodnight…]

VERNON *climbs in to a hammock.*

VERNON. Thanks for the best birthday present I ever had, Pelayo. Sixteen in the morning!

'Ting.' VERNON*'s in the bright lights of the big hotel.*

ACAPULCO CLERK (TAYLOR *in disguise*). Can I help you?

VERNON. Uh, I'm expecting a wire from Houston, Texas.

ACAPULCO CLERK. You have the password?

VERNON. No...

ACAPULCO CLERK. What's your name?

VERNON. Um... Vernon Little.

ACAPULCO CLERK. How much you expecting?

VERNON. Six hundred dollars.

ACAPULCO CLERK (*tapping her keyboard*). Nothing here.

VERNON. You sure?

She pops a party popper at VERNON.

TAYLOR. Freeze! Happy birthday, celebrity!

VERNON (*badly shaken*). Shit!

TAYLOR. You didn't wait for the wire details, like the password, dummy.

VERNON. Uh, so you hopped a fucken plane!

TAYLOR. Language, outlaw!

VERNON. Sorry. I can't believe you're here!

TAYLOR. Well, I couldn't leave you stranded. Anyway, I'm bummed back home and this is my vacation money. Here's three hundred, we'll work the math out later. I hope you don't mind sharing.

VERNON. I'll try to cope. How'd you know it's my birthday?

TAYLOR. Hell-o? The whole world knows it's your birthday, Vern! Come on, let's go upstairs.

VERNON. You booked a room, here?

TAYLOR. Twin room, so you better behave, serial killer, you.

VERNON. Wait up, Tay, I found the best place, somewhere you won't believe – a beach, with jungle, just wait till you see it –

TAYLOR. Eew! With, like, spiders and bugs? Eew! I already paid for the room, Vern, like, God. C'mon upstairs, you'll like it. C'mon.

There's a bed.

Hey, we're here now, snap out of it!

VERNON. Tay? You can see I ain't committing murders, right?

TAYLOR. Whoa, back up, I don't want to even, like, you know? I'm just here for – whatever.

VERNON. But, if they like…

TAYLOR. You ain't quitting, are ya, killer? Come to Tay-Tay, you bad boy.

She kicks off her shoes, starts undressing him.

VERNON. Uh, hold on, I can…

TAYLOR. Feeling shy? Taylor'll look after you.

She takes his hand, puts it under her shirt.

Feel nice?

VERNON. Uh, yeah….

She puts his other hand inside her skirt.

TAYLOR. And this – nice?

VERNON. Nice.

TAYLOR. I want to hear about you. Mm, that's good, higher. (*She wriggles out of her panties.*) Vernon, tell me some of the things you, urgh, did… Tell, urgh… tell me you did it for me…

VERNON. God, Tay, you're beautiful, I can't believe…

TAYLOR. Oh God, God, Christ, Vern, I'm… Vernon, you, ah, I'm, uuugh, God… (*She struggles, then submits.*) Ugh, fuck, no! Tell me what you did to those people, Vern! Tell me how you loved it, tell me you killed!

She starts to straighten her legs, draw away.

VERNON. It's okay, Tay, it's okay, ssshhh… it's okay…

TAYLOR. Did you do it for me, Vern? Tell me you did it for me.

VERNON (*whispering*). Yeah, sshh, I did it for you, Tay, I did it for you…

TAYLOR. Ha!

She scoots away, speaks in to her jacket.

Got it!

The door opens. A CAMERA CREW *come in, bright lights on* VERNON.

CAMERAMAN. Vernon Gregory Little?

VERNON. No, it's Patsy fucken Cline.

'Bye Bye Love' by Felice and Boudleaux Bryant.

CAMERA CREW (*singing*). Bye bye, love…

LALLY (*entering*). Well, hi.

VERNON. Shit.

CAMERA CREW (*singing*). Bye bye, happiness…

TAYLOR. Lally?

CAMERA CREW (*singing*). Hello, loneliness,
    I think I'm gonna cry…

TAYLOR. How did I do?

CAMERA CREW (*singing*). Bye bye, love…

TAYLOR. Anyone seen my panties?

CAMERA CREW (*singing*). Bye bye, sweet caress…

VERNON *is dressed in a blue prison suit and hog-tied with hand- and leg-cuffs.*

VERNON. Uuurgh…

CAMERA CREW (*singing*). Hello, emptiness,
  I feel like I could die,
  Goodbye, my love, goodbye…

TAYLOR. You said I could anchor the show?

LALLY. Why, sure…

He goes for a kiss, she rejects him.

TAYLOR. Contract.

LALLY (*singing*). There goes my baby,
  With someone new,
  She sure looks happy,
  I sure am blue,
  She was my baby,

  TAYLOR *gets fitted up with TV microphone, etc.*

  Till he stepped in,
  Goodbye to romance,
  That might have been…

The chorus underscores the following speech.

TAYLOR (*on TV*). Serial killer, Vernon Gregory Little, has been
  caught, discovered in a hotel room in Acapulco with media
  debutante, Taylor Figueroa. (*A cute smile.*) Flown in the
  early hours of last night to Houston, he was jeered by a huge
  crowd as he was led from the aircraft and harnessed into a
  security truck, which drove him, accompanied by eight
  helicopters and thirty police vehicles, to a prison cell, where
  he awaits trial.

  VERNON, *in his blue convict suit, is put in the court dock.*

VERNON. Mom?

MEDIA COURT OFFICER. She's not in court, dear. Okay, let's
  have a look at you. I should tell you, Mr Little, that there's no
  pressure whatsoever to press the buzzer, but if at any moment
  you should feel inclined to change your plea, or to revoke the

information given so far, the buzzer will give you recourse to
instant and positive action. It suits you, the blue! We'll just
grey-up the skin tones, put a bit more white on your lips –
you allergic to anything? Okay, let's go. Court arise for Judge
Nancy. Ladies and gentlemen, to camera please.

JUDGE. Court in session!

The PROSECUTOR *and* BRIAN *both have guitars. They
play them with increasing skill and speed to score points as
the scene progresses.*

PROSECUTOR. Welcome, ladies and gentlemen, to one of the
most cut-and-dried legal cases the state has ever seen.

BRIAN. Fellow citizens, how are you today?

PROSECUTOR. A case unprecedented, for the heartless, cold-
blooded evil, visited arbitrarily upon his victims.

BRIAN. Look at this meek, shy young man with no previous
record of wrongdoing. (*To* VERNON.) Brian Big, your
attorney, thrilled to meet you. (*Back to us.*) Take a long look.

PROSECUTOR. This is a human, and I use the term loosely,
who, at the tender age of sixteen, has extinguished the lives
of thirty-four citizens, the majority of them children.

BRIAN. This is a boy whose only mistake, and it was a big one,
was not to cry 'innocent!' loudly or clearly enough.

PROSECUTOR. And yet the boy cries 'innocent!' Not of one
crime, where perhaps his identity could've been mistaken,
but of all thirty-four vicious slayings he stands accused of!

MEDIA COURT OFFICER. First witness.

PROSECUTOR *hands* TAYLOR *a garishly bound Bible.*

PROSECUTOR. Ms Taylor Figueroa, good to see you. Have
you ever been stalked?

TAYLOR. I guess so. This guy just called up out of the blue and
started confessing to all these crimes and whatever.

PROSECUTOR. Where was this?

TAYLOR. Houston. He was on his way to, like, Mexico.

PROSECUTOR. Quite a detour.

TAYLOR. Mmm.

PROSECUTOR. Ms Figueroa, the defense claims that you knew Vernon Little was in Mexico when the sixteen most recent murders, of which he stands accused, took place across the state of Texas. Did you know he was there?

TAYLOR. Well, like, he was there when I arrived…

PROSECUTOR. For how long could you definitely say the defendant was in Mexico?

TAYLOR. Um, three hours, maybe, tops?

PROSECUTOR. What transpired during those hours with the accused in Mexico?

TAYLOR. He tried to, um, make out with me…

PROSECUTOR. Was this when he confessed?

TAYLOR. Uh-huh.

PROSECUTOR (*motioning for the tape to be played*). Please!

VERNON (*on tape*). *Yeah, sshh, I did it for you, Tay, I did it for you…*

PROSECUTOR (*to* BRIAN). All yours.

BRIAN. Ms Figueroa, why did Vernon Little meet you in Mexico?

TAYLOR. I guess he wanted to make out or confess or whatever.

BRIAN. You paid him to have sex with you?

TAYLOR. No!

BRIAN. So no money changed hands between you that day?

TAYLOR. Well…

BRIAN. 'Yes' or 'no' answers, please.

TAYLOR. See, but…

BRIAN. You gave Vernon Little money, yes or no?

TAYLOR. Yes.

BRIAN. Mn. How much?

TAYLOR. Uh…

BRIAN. We didn't hear that, how much money?

TAYLOR. Three hundred dollars.

BRIAN. Three hundred dollars, really? Darned boy must be
  good!

PROSECUTOR. Objection!

JUDGE. Sustained.

BRIAN. And finally, Miss Figueroa, tell us the name of the man
  who took you to Mexico?

TAYLOR. Eulalio Ledesma.

MEDIA COURT OFFICER. Next witness.

  LALLY *appears, takes the Bible.*

LALLY. I'm sorry to keep you waiting, ma'am, ladies and
  gentlemen – I had a meeting with the Secretary of State, you
  know how it is.

PROSECUTOR. Eulalio Ledesma, you have been in a unique
  position to observe the accused, being a close family friend
  and confidant, even living with the family, offering support
  in their time of need. Tell us, did you ever notice unusual or
  violent behaviour from Mr Little?

LALLY. God protect me, I did, yes, I'm afraid I did.

PROSECUTOR. Did he ever offer you illegal drugs?

LALLY. I'm afraid he did.

PROSECUTOR. Did he once invite you to discuss, forgive me, ladies and gentlemen, I quote, 'his granny's ass' with him?

LALLY. Lord forgive me, he did.

PROSECUTOR. And did the accused speak privately to you about the school tragedy?

LALLY. He talked in his sleep some nights – growled, more like. 'Boom,' he would say, 'Take that, booom…'

PROSECUTOR. I'm sorry to put you through this.

LALLY. Anything to bring peace upon those wretched souls… 'Let him who is without sin cast the first stone.'

PROSECUTOR. Amen. Mr Ledesma, you also witnessed Mr Little killing Sheriff Porkorney?

LALLY. From the ground where I lay injured I saw Vernon Little lift his gun, take aim, then I heard three shots. 'Forgive them, Lord, for they know not what they do.'

PROSECUTOR. Amen. Thank you for raking up that unhappy memory, Mr Ledesma.

LALLY. 'Blessed are the meek for they shall inherit the earth.'

EVERYBODY. Amen.

LALLY. 'And the Lord said come in to my boat, and they were amazed.'

EVERYBODY. Amen.

LALLY (*singing*). Amazing Grace…

BRIAN. Mr Ledesma, how long have you been a TV journalist?

LALLY (*singing*). How sweet…

BRIAN. Mr Ledesma?

LALLY (*singing*). The sound… (*Spoken.*) Ten years!

BRIAN. Ladies and gentlemen of the jury…

LALLY (*singing*). That saved…

BRIAN. Can everyone see this card?

LALLY (*singing*). A wretch…

He holds up LALLY's *repairman card.*

BRIAN. Mr Ledesma, is this your business card?

LALLY. No. (*Singing.*) Like me…

BRIAN. Your Honour, I'd like to append a witness to this examination, for the purpose of identification.

JUDGE. Go ahead.

LALLY (*singing*). I once…

LALLY'S MOM *rushes forward, stumbling, accompanied by* EILEENA.

BRIAN. Mrs Ledesma, thank you for joining us.

LALLY'S MOM. Lally?

LALLY (*singing*). Was lost…

JUDGE. Ma'am, can you point to your son?

LALLY'S MOM. Eulalio?

LALLY (*singing*). But now am found…

JUDGE. No, ma'am, I'm the Judge, can you identify your son?

LALLY'S MOM. Eu-lalio, where are you?

LALLY (*singing*). Was blind but now I see…

PROSECUTOR. Over here!

MEDIA COURT OFFICER. To camera.

LALLY'S MOM. You're not my Lallo.

The COURT *laughs.*

BRIAN. Objection!

JUDGE. Am I to understand your witness is visually impaired?

LALLY'S MOM. Lally?

PROSECUTOR. Mama!

The COURT *is in uproar.*

LALLY (*singing*). 'Twas grace that taught my heart to fear…

JUDGE. Counsel, take your witness away!

LALLY (*singing*). And grace my fears relieved…

JUDGE. Order, order, order, order!

She keeps on calling for order, to no avail.

LALLY (*singing*). How precious did that grace appear,
The hour I first believed.

JUDGE. Motherfuckers!

The COURT *is finally silent.*

MEDIA COURT OFFICER. Next witness.

PROSECUTOR. Dr Goosens, as a psychiatrist, do Mr Little's
crimes suggest a pattern to you?

DR GOOSENS (*with the Bible*). They do. They are the patterns
of a psychopath.

PROSECUTOR. Thank you. All yours.

BRIAN. Dr Goosens, heard of the internet site 'Bambi Boy Butt
Bazaar?'

PROSECUTOR. Objection!

JUDGE. Proceed, but feel free to get to the point.

BRIAN. I have exhibits here showing that you, Oliver Goosens,
were charged in Oklahoma for procuring and corrupting
teenage boys for this website, which you own and operate
still, and which previously went under the name of 'Teenage
Tools for Tom, Dick and Harry'.

DR GOOSENS. May I just say...

PROSECUTOR. Objection!

BRIAN. And, Dr Goosens, I propose that you were treating
Jesus Navarro twice weekly in the run-up to the school
tragedy in May this year.

VERNON. Treating Jesus?

BRIAN. And, what's more, that you presented young Jesus with
ladies' undergarments, a charge for the purchase of which
has been traced to your credit card, and that you
photographed him wearing those undergarments and posted a
pornographic picture of him on 'Bambi Boy Butt Bazaar' the
very night before the tragedy!

PROSECUTOR. Objection!

VERNON. Stop, stop, please stop!

JUDGE. Please keep your client quiet. Counsel, it is not the
Doctor who is on trial here! Ladies and gentlemen of the
jury, you are hereby instructed to ignore this evidence.

VERNON. Excuse me?

JUDGE. Next witness.

VERNON. No, you don't understand...

JUDGE. Silence!

   VERNON *reaches for the buzzer. There is a hush and a
   whirr of cameras.*

BRIAN. Vernon, no!

   It chimes loudly, like an airplane xylophone.

JUDGE. Mr Little, you wish to change your plea?

VERNON. You don't understand about Dr Goosens.

JUDGE. Why did you ring the buzzer, if you don't want to
change your plea?

VERNON. I know what happened, I know what happened to Jesus now, if he was being treated by / him –

BRIAN (*simultaneous*). Vernon...

PROSECUTOR (*simultaneous*). The State would hope to preserve the structure of the case, Your Honour, after all the work that's gone in to it.

JUDGE. Two minutes, counsel.

BRIAN. Oh oh....

PROSECUTOR. I appreciate it, Your Honour.

PROSECUTOR *gives* VERNON *the Bible, he bats it away, distressed. There's a gasp from the court.*

LALLY *and* EVERYBODY (*singing*).
The world shall soon dissolve like snow...

PROSECUTOR. Your position, Mr Little, is that you weren't even in Texas when the murders took place, correct?

LALLY *and* EVERYBODY (*singing*). The sun refuse to shine...

VERNON. No.

PROSECUTOR. Where were you?

VERNON. Mexico. But, sir, Dr Goosens –

PROSECUTOR. You were in Mexico on the 20th of May this year?

LALLY *and* EVERYBODY (*singing*). But God, who called me...

VERNON. No, that was the day of the tragedy...

PROSECUTOR. But you just told this court you were in Mexico at the time of the murders.

VERNON. The recent ones...

PROSECUTOR. Ah, you went to Mexico for some of the murders, that's your story now?

VERNON. No, I meant...

LALLY *and* EVERYBODY (*singing*). Here below...

PROSECUTOR. And where were you when you weren't in Mexico?

VERNON. At home.

PROSECUTOR. Which is in the vicinity of the Keeters' property, where the body of Sheriff Porkorney was found. You're the closest known associate of the gunman, Jesus Navarro, you went to school at the scene of seventeen of the homicides, you have been identified at all of the murders. When first interviewed, you abscond, when released on bail, you run to Mexico –

LALLY *and* EVERYBODY (*singing*). Shall be forever mine.

PROSECUTOR. Where exactly were you in Mexico, Vernon Little?

VERNON. Guerrero. My friend, Pelayo, can tell you.

PROSECUTOR. The truck driver from the village on the coast?

VERNON. Yes, Pelayo!

PROSECUTOR (*picking up a document*). The sworn affidavit of Pelayo Garcia-Madero from Guerrero. Mr Garcia-Madero states that he only ever met one American youth in his life. He met him in a bar, drove him to the south of Mexico in his truck. His name was Brad Pritchard.

VERNON. Yes, that's me, that's just the name I gave him!

There's a scuffle at the back of the court. MR ABDINI *is physically restrained from entering.*

LALLY *and* EVERYBODY (*singing*). I once was lost but now am found...

MR ABDINI (*shouting*). Tell them about the poo-poos, Bernom, tell them about the poo-poos!

MEDIA COURT OFFICER. To camera, everybody!

VERNON. Where's Mr Nuckles? Ask Mr Nuckles!

MR ABDINI (*down the corridor*). He just a baby! Tell them about the poop!

VERNON. I didn't do anything!

LALLY *and* EVERYBODY (*singing*). Was blind but now I see…

MEDIA COURT OFFICER. As an accessory to murder in the first degree of seventeen school children at Martirio High – Max Lechuga…

As we hear their names, we see school photos of the children grinning at the camera, and hear a soundtrack of what happened that day in VERNON's *memory.*

MAX (*voice-over*). Jesus! Meskin-Bambi-boy!

LORI (*voice-over*). Leave him alone, Max!

MEDIA COURT OFFICER. Charlotte Brewster…

MAX (*voice-over*). He your friend coz he look like a big girl? Won't make a grab for your muff, huh, Lori?

MEDIA COURT OFFICER. Madonna Black, Stephen Burger…

MAX (*voice-over*). Hey, Jesus, come show Lori your muff and your titties, hrr!

MEDIA COURT OFFICER. Beau Gurie…

BEAU GURIE (*voice-over*). Show us your little red panties, Jesus…

MEDIA COURT OFFICER. Grace Richly, McFadden Hunt…

MAX (*voice-over*). Sir, I can't be in class with a porn queen.

CHARLOTTE (*voice-over*). Yeah, sir…

MEDIA COURT OFFICER. Eric Priestley, Randy Norton…

CHARLOTTE (*voice-over*). We have a right to be protected from deviated sexual influences.

MEDIA COURT OFFICER. Rachel Newman, Henry Carter…

BEAUX GURIE (*voice-over*). We might catch his disease…

MEDIA COURT OFFICER. Miles Handley, Richie Chew, Mary White…

MAX (*voice-over*). Googled any retarded Meskins lately, sir? Taken a look at them gay-boy sites?

CHARLOTTE *and* OTHERS (*voice-over*). Tee hee hee hee.

MEDIA COURT OFFICER. Bob Pointer, Suzzie Sledgeman…

MAX (*voice-over*). Like, number thirty-four on 'Bambi Boy Butt Bazaar'…

BEAU GURIE (*voice-over*). Nice panties, but next time shave your ass, Jesus.

MAX (*voice-over*). Meskins are real hairy…

EVERYBODY (*voice-over*). Hurgh hurgh hurgh hurgh…

MAX (*voice-over*). Look, sir, look!

The class hoots and cheers.

Look at porn star Jesus!

BEAU GURIE (*voice-over*). Jesus, you dirty bitch!

Jeering from the whole class.

MEDIA COURT OFFICER. And Lori Donner. How do you find the defendant?

FOREMAN. Guilty, guilty, guilty.

JESUS is there, with his face shot away. The court has gone,
VERNON is alone. MOM, at home, sings 'Please Help Me
I'm Falling' by Hank Locklin. VERNON speaks to MOM,
although she can't hear him.

N. The way he ran from class, I knew the storm was
ing in Jesus. He'd been wired for weeks, more ditzy
than usual, calling it love but not saying who with... If you'd
come to Houston, Mom, and been in court you'd have heard
about the photo on the Doctor's website. That morning in
math, this picture of Jesus in these stupid panties, was on
every computer in the room. 'Bambi Boy Butt Bazaar'? He
had no idea. He jackknifed. I asked Lori to cover for me
because I knew where he was headed. I raced to Keeter's on
my bike, to the den, where both our daddy's guns were. He
wasn't there. The den was locked, my key at home. I saw
through the crack in the door, Daddy's rifle was there, not
moved since the day we left it, but his daddy's had gone. My
turn to jackknife. Back on the bike, my insides cramped, what
a surprise. Gastro-enteritis fuckin' Little. I squatted, emptied
my lower tracts like rats from an airplane, right beside the
den. *'Tell them about the poo-poos!'* says my attorney, and
he's right. They'd know I wasn't in school, then. You'd know
I wasn't in school too, but what am I supposed to say? 'Sure,
there's the shit, right beside my papa's grave where me an'
Mom buried him in the middle of the fucking night after she
shot him dead. And in case you're interested, the gun's right
behind that corrugated door. The key? Sure – little box in my
room – anything else I can help with?' My shit makes me
innocent but it sure as hell would put you away. Seventeen
children? How could you think I did that?

By the time I cleaned myself up, Jesus was at school with his
pop's loaded rifle. I didn't get there in time. I found his bag
outside the classroom, picked it up, held onto it. Inside was
another round of ammunition beside his lunch – shrimp-
paste on white. I looked through the door and there they all
were – shot to pieces, and there was my goofy friend Jesus,
with the gun pointing deep inside his mouth.

VERNON *is on Death Row, in his cell. He is passive,
lumpen, barely alive. His fellow* CONVICTS *are equally
dulled.* LALLY*'s theme tune spills from the TV. It's highly
polished these days.*

LEONA (*on TV*). And now for a man at the cutting edge of television. A man who has developed a truly democratic system, where the public can influence which criminals they spend their taxes supporting. For the first time in history, cameras will be allowed in to Death Row so viewers can judge the prisoners for themselves. Public voting is the brainchild of Ledesma Empires and we are honoured to have in our studio this morning – Eulalio Ledesma, welcome!

LALLY (*on TV*). Leona-Peaches, hi.

VERNON *twitches involuntarily, spasms through his body as the news reports progress.*

LEONA. Your point, Eulalio, is that not so long ago all executions were public?

LALLY (*on TV*). Held in the town square, even, and guess what? Crimes went down, public satisfaction, up. Public voting on criminals makes sense at every level. Criminals cost money, popular TV makes money. What we're looking at here is reality TV empowering the public, giving them a real chance to have their say. It's giving people what they want.

MOM (*on phone*). Vernon?

JONESY *turns the volume right down on the TV.* LEONA *and* LALLY *carry on talking in mute.*

VERNON. Mom?

MOM. Vernon? Well, we can see you on the television… Why do you look so impassive, Vernon?

VERNON. Beats me, Mom.

MOM. Well, you look strange, and people will be voting soon.

PAM (*on phone*). Vern, it's Pam, you get my Valentine's?

VERNON. It's up in my cell. Thank you.

PAM. D'you get any others or have they all forgotten ya?

VERNON. One other.

PAM. Who from?

VERNON. Ella Keeter.

PAM. Keeter's kid? Lord! What're they feedin' ya?

VERNON. Uh, feeding me?

JONESY. Chorizo and egg.

VERNON. Chorizo and egg.

PAM. That's it, just chorizo and egg?

VERNON. Uh…

JONESY. Hash browns, ice cream, relish, oysters… whatever the hell you want.

VERNON. Don't worry, Pam, I'm eating.

> JONESY *turns the TV volume back on. A burst of* LALLY *music.* VERNON*'s talk-time is up.*

TAYLOR (*on TV*). Is this the end of the road for serial killer, Vernon Gregory Little?

VERNON. Pam, I gotta go.

TAYLOR (*on TV*). Vernon and his psychopath boyfriend, Jesus Navarro, went on a killing spree, murdering seventeen of their school friends in the small Texan town of Martirio. Vernon Little, along with two other convicts, will be on your screens 24/7, with cameras inside the walls of Death Row for the first time in prison history, for you to decide if this is the week his life will end.

> VERNON*'s spasms evolve in to line-dancing moves in an anarchic, volatile fashion, repeating sections of dance over and over again.* TAYLOR*'s report is simultaneous with the following scene.*

The idea has been so successful there's a bidding-war between top TV companies to buy broadcast rights to the executions. Any minute now we'll be going in live to Death Row to see how Vernon Little and fellow convicts are getting along. You can vote by phone, internet or text. For more information, log on to deathrow.com. The last shall go first, you decide who! This is Taylor Figueroa, live on five.

CON ONE (*over the report*). Jeezus, Little, fuck up with yer cunted noise!

VERNON*'s mad dance continues.*

Burnem Little, what's wrong wit' you, man?

VERNON*'s dancing increases in fury.*

CON TWO. He losin' it.

CON ONE. You motherfuckin' scroted cunt-ass shitsucker!

JONESY. Je-sus Ch-risst, keep it down, willya?

CON ONE. Then shut him the fuck up, squeakin' that way on the fuckin' floor!

JONESY. Chill out, the kid's entitled to a little diversion...

CON ONE. I ain't kiddin', Jonesy, that squeak, squeak, squeaky's killing me!

CON TWO. He need some therapy, man.

CON ONE. Fix him some time with Lasalle.

JONESY. Yeah, like you guys give the orders round here.

CON TWO. He needs to face his God.

JONESY. Take more'n talkin' to straighten this boy out...

CON ONE. I have some basic goddam human rights in this fuckin' joint!

JONESY. Goddammit, I'll see what I can do.

VERNON *stops moving.*

CON ONE. Thank the Lord in Heaven, sweet fuckin' silence.

VERNON. Jonesy, who's Lasalle?

JONESY. Never you mind, son.

VERNON *starts his furious dance again.*

CON ONE. Aw, no, no, no, no, no, not the fucking squeakin',
fuck / me!

JONESY. Calm down, will / ya?

CON ONE. With that cunting noise? Jus' take the kid to the
basement, Jonesy!

JONESY. Mr Ledesma ordered no more visits…

CON ONE *joins in the manic dancing.*

CON ONE (*shouting*). Okay, Jonesy, okay, okay, if this is the
way you fuckin' want it!

CON TWO *cottons on, joins in too, making as much noise as
possible. It sets off the whole prison, it's group anarchy.*

CON ONE, CON TWO *and* OTHER CONS. Squeaky squeaky
fucken squeaky, this ain't gonna stop, never gonna stop, take
him to Lasalle, take him, take him, fucken take him… (*Etc.*)

JONESY. Shit, okay, okay, get ready!

They all stop dancing.

Jesus wept.

CON ONE. Yo, Burnam, learnin' how to git along!

VERNON. Who's Lasalle?

JONESY (*unlocking a door*). Pastor Lasalle.

VERNON. You lock the Pastor in here?

JONESY. I lock you in here.

LASALLE*'s scary, in a wheelchair.*

LASALLE. Crusty young outcast, lopin' away to hop another
bus outta town. Only one bus leaves these parts, son, an' you
know where it's goin'.

VERNON. Excuse me?

LASALLE. Know why you down here with me?

VERNON. No.

LASALLE. Only one reason, boy, you ain't faced your God.

VERNON. How d'you know that?

LASALLE. Because I'm human. How you feel about us humans?

VERNON. Not much. They're all – excuse my language, Pastor – fucked.

LASALLE. Boy, ain't that the truth, amen. Sounds to me like you plain don't want to associate wit' people no more, rather not be around them.

VERNON. You're right there, Pastor.

LASALLE. Well, you got your wish. What else you wish for, son? I bet you dreamed of quittin' home?

VERNON. I guess…

LASALLE. Presto, you looking more and more lucky.

VERNON. What kind of logic's that?

LASALLE. Ah, so you a logical boy? You all strung out on everybody else's lies and behaviours that you hate. You busy standing around thinking to yourself, 'Why, that ain't right, that can't be that way!' I bet you can't even tell me a thing you love.

VERNON *is silent.*

You have a poppa?

VERNON. No, sir. Used to.

LASALLE. A momma?

VERNON. Yeah.

LASALLE. Let me guess, she the kind of lady make you feel guilty about the leastest lil thing? 'If you could jus' get ye'self a job'…

VERNON. You meet her, or somethin'?

LASALLE. I told you, I'm human. She guilts you up then sits right back and lets you suffer, huh?

VERNON. Yep.

LASALLE. If she came with a user's guide it'd tell you to fuck her off in the end, am I right?

VERNON. Um, yeah.

LASALLE. Boy, that woman must be one stupid cunt. Must be the dumbest fuckin' snatch-rag that ever roamed this earth. Probably is so butt-spastic…

VERNON. Hey, hey, you sure you're a pastor?

LASALLE. Boy, she one selfish fuckin' piss-flap…

VERNON. Don't fucken talk like that about my mom!

LASALLE. No love, huh, kid? Face it, you messed up.

VERNON. But, Pastor, I never – (*He stops.*)

LASALLE. Never what, thought beyond blaming the people you love? How d'you think she feel about herself?

VERNON. She feels shit-brown about herself.

LASALLE. 'Any boy of mine must crack out the same shit-brown mould I come from…'

A burst of TV noise in the background, simultaneous with the scene, as LALLY flies in.

TAYLOR (*on TV*). And we're just gathering in the last of the votes to learn who is dying today. One hundred and eighty-nine million, at the last count! And… all the votes are in now… that's a record-breaking two hundred million votes!

LALLY (*simultaneous with above*). What's going on here, aren't the men supposed to be segregated?

JONESY. Oh sure, it's just a little counselling makes the living easier up on the Row…

LALLY. These cells are out of bounds, we're installing post-production down here.

VERNON. How's your mama, Mr Laid-his-ma?

LALLY *lunges for* VERNON *but stops himself.*

JONESY. Jesus, kid!

VERNON. Go on, show 'em your nice side, Daddy Lally.

LASALLE *chuckles darkly.*

TAYLOR (*on TV*). Stay tuned in while we count the convict out!

LALLY. Votes're being processed.

He drinks some ginseng, leaves.

Good luck, big man.

VERNON. Jonesy, can I have another minute? Please?

JONESY. Just one.

LASALLE*'s wheeling away.*

VERNON. Lasalle?

LASALLE. Shit! What you think I can do for you on some poor bastard's execution day?

VERNON. That's the point, it might be mine, so, like – help me face my God?

LASALLE. Git on you knees, make a wish, you a free man? Officer Jones, any news on the boy's pardon?

VERNON. Some preacher you are, face God yourself!

LASALLE. Blind, dumb shit, what God? You think a caring intelligence would wipe out babies from hunger, watch decent folk scream, burn and bleed every second of the night and day? That ain't no God, that's just people! You stuck with the rest of us in this snake-pit of human wants, frustrated and calcified into needs, achin' and raw...

VERNON. I didn't even do anything!

LASALLE. So don't come crying to me coz you stood in the way of another man's needs!

VERNON *is silenced.*

Why you think the world chewin' off its own legs? Becausen we're promised the goodies, we can see the meat, but we can't fucken get it. We is all underdogs in the great big meat market for promises.

VERNON. Underdogs? Yeah, especially him... (*Referring to* LALLY.)

LASALLE. Especially him. A dog on the trail o' blood.

VERNON. So what did you mean, that I ain't faced my God?

LASALLE. I'll make it first grade, so's even fuckin you can understand. Papa God growed us up till we could wear long pants then licensed his name to dollar bills, left some car keys on the table and got the fuck outta town. Us fallible puppies is the only holy bein' you ever gonna find. It's your choice. You a dog or a God? You choose.

A bell tolls.

JONESY. Time for the final event.

VERNON *thinks he's there for him, but* JONESY *takes hold of* LASALLE.

VERNON. Lasalle... you're a convict?

LASALLE. Not for much longer, looks like.

VERNON. But... but...

LASALLE. There ain't no morals, no justice, just chaos. A dog chases meat, a God dangles meat, that's all. Know folk's needs, son, they'll dance to any fuckin' tune you sing.

VERNON. But what if it's too late?

LASALLE. Son, you heard the true way to mourn the dead?

VERNON. No.

LASALLE. Take care of the living, it's all you have.

JONESY. That's enough, Lasalle.

LASALLE. It's never too late. Time to be your true God-self, kid, give the people what they want.

VERNON. But...

LASALLE. Shit, you suckin' the last drop of milk from me here... You know what meat is! See these boys, all tough and gnarled? (*Re: fellow convicts*.) Know what they's wantin'?

VERNON. Freedom?

LASALLE. Nu-uh. (*Instructing* JONESY *to play a note*.) Jonesy? (*To* VERNON.) Listen.

LASALLE starts to sing 'Bye Bye Blackbird' by Ray Henderson and Mort Dixon, very softly. The CONS follow LASALLE's lead, responding to his sung calls, singing gently as lambs in their own cells.

All they dogs wantin', Vernon God Little, is tenderness. Don't go in swinging no axe – I made some mistakes in ma time... Jus' give.

VERNON. Thank you.

LASALLE. No, thank you, Vernon God.

JONESY. Get yoursel' ready, Lasalle.

LASALLE. I'm ready. Shit, I'm ready now.

The CONS resume their song. It crescendos to a full and beautiful finale, LASALLE's voice soaring out over the CONS' as he climbs out of his wheelchair up to his gurney.

VERNON. See you, Lasalle.

News music.

TAYLOR (*on TV*). And that was goodbye to axe murderer, Clarence Lasalle, what a guy. This week we choose between

Sven the killer from Kansas, Bohemian Bobby, and, of course, the murdering maniac from Martirio, Vernon Gregory Little.

LASALLE (*a memory*). Give the people what they want, Vernon God...

MOM (*a memory*). Even murderers are loved by their families, you know.

TAYLOR (*on TV*). And, the votes are nearly in, an amazing two hundred and eighty-six million votes! No – three hundred million, an all-time max! And our systems are busy counting the final few, and... yes, we have a winner!

It's quiet. VERNON *is alone in his cell.*

CON ONE. Burnem, you okay, my man?

JONESY (*coming in*). We need to get you changed now.

VERNON. Jonesy, can I do it myself, for once...?

JONESY *gives him his clothes.* VERNON *undresses, puts his Mexican clothes back on, gives his trainers to* JONESY.

Could you give these to cell five for me?

CON ONE. Yo, Burnem, fuck 'em up, man, piss on those muthas...

VERNON. Thanks, man. Jordan New Jacks, I've tread some miles in those shoes.

CON ONE. Yo. Maybe I'll take up the squeak-squeak routine.

JONESY *brings in supper.*

JONESY. Your last supper has been supervised by a lady called – 'Pam'. 'Chik'n'Mix Choice Supreme, with fries, rib-rings, corn relish and two tubs o' coleslaw.' Never liked coleslaw myself.

VERNON. Me neither, but my mom says it's good for you, so.

JONESY. Pam were picky about stuffin' bread in the tub to absorb the steam.

LASALLE (*a memory*). Know folk's needs, son, and they'll dance to any fuckin' tune you sing.

VERNON. Jonesy, I ain't hungry, do I get a phone call instead?

JONESY. Sure.

VERNON. Or a bunch?

JONESY. You got three minutes.

LALLY (*on phone*). Ledesma Empires?

VERNON. It's Vern.

LALLY. Big man, not dead yet?

VERNON. Want to know where my gun is?

LALLY. Talk to me.

VERNON. You'll find the key to our den in my room. Take it to the old quarry by Keeter's, it's all yours.

JONESY. Two minutes, Little.

TAYLOR (*on phone*). Tayla?

VERNON. It's Vern. I know you need a big story break to boost your TV career, so – be at Keeter's, old quarry, tonight, with a camera crew.

JONESY. One minute.

VAINE (*on phone*). Vaine Gurie?

VERNON. Ma'am, a hero of the law is needed tonight to protect the world from a homocidal maniac, if you're interested.

JONESY. Thirty seconds.

VERNON. Mom?

MOM (*on phone, not coping*). Vernon… have you used the bathroom today?

VERNON. Mom, can you say goodbye to Pam and Nana for me?

MOM. Well, Vernon, I haven't told your nana about the trouble, she's old and she only watches shopping, she won't have seen the news…

VERNON. What about when I don't show up for lawn-mowing this spring?

JONESY. Time's up, Little.

VERNON. And, Mom?

MOM. Yes, Vernon?

The phone clicks off.

VERNON. Even murderers are loved by their families, you know…

JONESY. He's too small.

An OFFICER fetches a block for VERNON to stand on so he fits the gurney. JESUS is there, calm, a bit cleaned up.

VERNON. Jeezus. Do we all die this quietly?

JONESY. We need a signature on this waiver here, that's it.

He gets VERNON to sign.

Anaesthetic.

An OFFICER slides a needle in to his arm.

Expect to feel a form of euphoria, which will last until the final injection. Bye, son.

JONESY plays 'I'll Fly Away' by Albert E Brumley, on the harmonica. VERNON lifts up, high above us.

VERNON (*to* JESUS). End-of-the-road music, it had to be. Those country dudes. All they sing 'bout is the trouble they're in, the shit they seen… I thought I'd play out to angry poetry, Eminem, maybe, but that 'tss, tss, tss'– boosts you up, convinces you you're gonna win, then when the song's over you discover, oh, you fucken lost. Anyway, too late now, all of it. (*To us.*) What? You still looking at me? You'll have to find

yourselves some other booger-sack of a loser to look at now.
Pack up your philosophical activity set, Vernon Gonad...

MOM *and* PAM *are sitting on the sofa.* MOM *is crying and
singing,* PAM *is singing.*

PAM *and* MOM (*singing*).
  One bright morning, when this life is over,
  I'll fly away,
  To a home on God's celestial shore,
  I'll fly away,
  I'll fly away, oh glory,
  I'll fly away, in the morning,
  When I die, hallelujah...

LALLY *arrives in* VERNON's *bedroom.*

LALLY. Come on, where's this fucking key...? Got the bastard!

TAYLOR (*a memory*). Nasty acid, nasty, nasty gels...

  LALLY *finds the bottle, drinks it.*

LALLY. Thanks for the ginseng, big man!

  The acid kicks in.

  Woo!

  From a helicopter above.

TAYLOR. Just circle overhead, boys, until I say the word.
  Okay, let's shoot.

  LALLY's *at the den.*

LALLY. Lally's comin' to get you, little gun, little gun, king of
  TV, king of the fucken world's headin' your way!

LASALLE *and* JESUS (*singing*).
  When the shadows of this life have gone,
  I'll fly away,
  Like a bird from prison bars has flown,
  I'll fly away,
  I'll fly away, oh glory, I'll fly away,

When I die, hallelujah, by and by,
I'll fly away…

LALLY*'s tripping completely now.*

LALLY. Gotcha! Gotcha, gotcha, gotcha, gotcha, gunny, gunny, gotcha… (*Etc.*)

VAINE. This is the police!

LALLY. Mami? Mama?

VAINE. This is the police, drop the gun!

LALLY*'s reeling in a wild circle.*

LALLY. Mama!

TAYLOR. Keep it steady, boys, keep shooting.

VAINE. You heard me! Drop the gun, or I'll shoot!

TAYLOR. Keep shooting.

VAINE. I'll shoot!

LALLY *finds the trigger and shoots arbitrarily. A scream from the helicopter.*

TAYLOR. Fuck! Oh my God, he shot me in the ass! Aahhhh, shit!

VAINE. Open fire!

She shoots, in her element at last – 'Bam, bam, bam, bam, bam.' LALLY *dances as he's riddled with bullets, reminiscent of* VERNON*'s line-dance on Death Row.*

LALLY. Ass-biscuits.

He finally thuds, twitching, to the ground. MR ABDINI *bursts in to the execution chamber, waving a brown lump.*

MR ABDINI. Testa prove it, eets your poo-poos!

JONESY. His what?

MR ABDINI. His poop, his poo-poo, I found his facetious!

He holds it up. The music stops, everyone stops, nobody breathes.

JONESY. But… you're too late.

Everyone is silent, stunned.

No, wait a goddam minute, he's still on the anaesthetic! Little, your pardon came through! Little? Little? Come back to us, now. I promise you won't have to eat coleslaw…

EVERYBODY (*singing*). I'll fly away, oh glory,
  I'll fly away, in the morning,
  When I die, hallelujah, by and by,
  I'll fly away.

VERNON *is brought down from the gurney to cheers from the* CONS *and everybody.*

VERNON. Hi, Mom.

MOM. Oh, dear Lord in Heaven… (*She diverts her emotion.*) It's here, Vernon, the special-edition refrigerator's arrived!

VERNON. Hi, Pam.

PAM. Is that the colour you ordered?

VERNON. Thanks for looking after Mom.

PAM. Any time, little Vern. We liked your picture on the front cover of *Time* magazine – 'Stool's Out!' Haugh, haugh, haugh, haugh!

VAINE *comes on, confident, with a gun in a holster.*

VAINE. Hello, Vernon.

VERNON. Hi, Vaine. Congratulations on your promotion.

VAINE. Just doing my job, is all. Hi, girls.

MOM. Hi, Vaine.

PAM. Neat spectacles.

VAINE. Not too showy?

PAM. Lord no, very Clint Eastwood.

MOM. Coke, Vaine?

MR ABDINI. Biernom! Hello, everybody!

MOM. Oh, Mr Abdini!

MR ABDINI. Mrs Biernom!

MOM. Can I get you a drink?

MR ABDINI. Thank you, Mrs Biernom. Do you have a cock?

We hear a snatch of 'He'll Keep his Word' approaching.
ELLA *appears.*

ELLA. Hi, Bernie.

VERNON. Ella! Did you remember the flowers?

ELLA. Course I did. (*Calling.*) Daddy? We picked the whole
field!

MR KEETER *brings on armfuls of wildflowers.*

MR KEETER. Okay, son?

VERNON. Wow, thank you, sir!

MR KEETER *dumps the flowers on the ground.*

MR KEETER. Some turnaround, how d'you get out of that
one?

VERNON. I guess I just faced my God.

MR KEETER. Your daddy'd be proud, if he weren't worm food
in my quarry.

ELLA. Daddy!

VAINE. He can rest in peace, Mr Keeter, now we know who
fired the gun that killed him. I don't know what Mr Ledesma
held against him, but anyway, he's worm food too.

VERNON *turns to* MR KEETER.

VERNON. Mr Keeter? I'd like you to meet my mom, Doris.

MR KEETER. Doris? A fine-looking heifer.

VAINE *clears her throat.*

MOM. Take a seat, Mr Keeter.

MR KEETER. Call me – Xavier.

He sits next to MOM *on the sofa.* VERNON *goes to pick up the flowers.*

PAM. What are the flowers for, Vern, the graves?

VERNON. No. They're for Jesus's mom.

EVERYBODY. Oh.

VERNON. Just trying to take care of the living.

ELLA kneels to help him sort the flowers. They find each other's hands. Everyone watches as they move tentatively towards a first kiss. Up high, no longer haunting him, is JESUS, *singing 'Crazy'.*

PAM. Eat up, Vern!

Flowers cascade over VERNON *and* ELLA *as they kiss.*

CURTAIN CALL

VERNON *and* ELLA *start to line-dance together, while still kissing, to 'May the Circle be Unbroken'. Everyone joins in the song and the dance.*

The End.

The following doubling was used in the Young Vic production in 2011 for the cast of ten actors:

Vernon

Jesus

Mom

Vaine / Leona / Team Leader / Chrissie / Media Court Officer

Sheriff Porkorney / Brad / Mr Keeter / Mr Deutschman / Bartender / Prosecutor / Jonesy

Pam / Judge Helen Gurie / May-May / Little Old Lady / Border Guard / Pelayo's Wife / Judge

Lally

Ella / Taylor / Eileena / Acapulco Clerk

Lasalle / Dr Goosens / Court Officer / Kid In Braces / Lally's Mom / Steven / Bus Driver / Pelayo

Mr Abdini / Pastor Gibbons / Heavy / Todd / Silas / Brian / Cameraman / Con One

Other characters to be played by members of the company.

Acknowledgements

The author and publisher gratefully acknowledge permission to quote from the following song lyrics: **'Bye Bye, Love'** by Felice Bryant/Boudleaux Bryant. © Sony/ATV Acuff Rose Music. All Rights Reserved. **'Galveston'** by Jimmy Webb. © 1968 Jobete Music Co. Inc., USA. Reproduced by permission of Jobeter Music Co. Inc./EMI Music Publishing Ltd, London WC2H 0QY. **'I'll Fly Away'** by A.E. Brumley. © Integrated Copyright Group, Inc. Published by Kobalt Music Publishing Ltd.

Ariel Dorfman
DEATH AND THE MAIDEN
PURGATORIO
READER
THE RESISTANCE TRILOGY
WIDOWS

Helen Edmundson
ANNA KARENINA *after* Tolstoy
THE CLEARING
CORAM BOY *after* Gavin
GONE TO EARTH *after* Webb
LIFE IS A DREAM *after* Calderón
THE MILL ON THE FLOSS *after* Eliot
MOTHER TERESA IS DEAD
ORESTES *after* Euripides
WAR AND PEACE *after* Tolstoy

Debbie Tucker Green
BORN BAD
DIRTY BUTTERFLY
RANDOM
STONING MARY
TRADE & GENERATIONS

Fin Kennedy
HOW TO DISAPPEAR COMPLETELY
AND NEVER BE FOUND
PROTECTION
THE URBAN GIRL'S GUIDE TO CAMPING *and other plays*

Liz Lochhead
BLOOD AND ICE
DRACULA *after* Bram Stoker
EDUCATING AGNES ('The School for Wives') *after* Molière
GOOD THINGS
MARY QUEEN OF SCOTS GOT HER HEAD CHOPPED OFF
MEDEA *after* Euripides
MISERYGUTS & TARTUFFE *after* Molière
PERFECT DAYS
THEBANS

Ayub Khan-Din
EAST IS EAST
LAST DANCE AT DUM DUM
NOTES ON FALLING LEAVES
RAFTA, RAFTA…

Lucy Kirkwood
BEAUTY AND THE BEAST *with* Katie Mitchell
BLOODY WIMMIN
HEDDA *after* Ibsen
IT FELT EMPTY WHEN THE HEART WENT AT FIRST BUT IT
IS ALRIGHT NOW
TINDERBOX

Tony Kushner
ANGELS IN AMERICA – PARTS ONE & TWO
CAROLINE OR CHANGE
HOMEBODY/KABUL

Tracy Letts
AUGUST: OSAGE COUNTY

Conor McPherson
DUBLIN CAROL
McPHERSON: FOUR PLAYS
McPHERSON PLAYS: TWO
PORT AUTHORITY
THE SEAFARER
SHINING CITY
THE WEIR

Arthur Miller
AN ENEMY OF THE PEOPLE *after* Ibsen
PLAYING FOR TIME

Brett Neveu
RED BUD

Bruce Norris
CLYBOURNE PARK
THE PAIN AND THE ITCH

Nina Raine
THE DRUNKS
from Mikhail *and* Vyacheslav Durnenkov
RABBIT
TRIBES

Tanya Ronder
BLOOD WEDDING *after* Lorca
PERIBANEZ *after* Lope de Vega

Polly Teale
AFTER MRS ROCHESTER
BRONTË
JANE EYRE *after* Brontë
MINE
SPEECHLESS *with* Linda Brogan

Lawrence Till
KES *after* Hines

Enda Walsh
BEDBOUND & MISTERMAN
DELIRIUM
DISCO PIGS & SUCKING DUBLIN
ENDA WALSH PLAYS: ONE
THE NEW ELECTRIC BALLROOM
PENELOPE
THE SMALL THINGS
THE WALWORTH FARCE

Nicolas Wright
CRESSIDA
HIS DARK MATERIALS
after Pullman
MRS KLEIN
THERESE RAQUIN
after Zola
THE REPORTER
VINCENT IN BRIXTON
WRIGHT: FIVE PLAYS

A Nick Hern Book

This stage adaptation of *Vernon God Little* first published in Great Britain as a paperback original in 2007 by Nick Hern Books Limited, 14 Larden Road, London W3 7ST, in association with the Young Vic

Reprinted in this revised edition 2011

Stage adaptation of *Vernon God Little* copyright © 2007, 2011 Tanya Ronder

Tanya Ronder has asserted her right to be identified as the author of this work

Cover design by Ned Hoste, 2H

Typeset by Nick Hern Books, London
Printed and bound in Great Britain by CPI Bookmarque, Croydon, Surrey

A CIP catalogue record for this book is available from the British Library

ISBN 978 1 84842 173 8

Mixed Sources
Product group from well-managed forests and other controlled sources
www.fsc.org Cert no. TT-COC-002227
© 1996 Forest Stewardship Council
FSC